WITHDRAWN

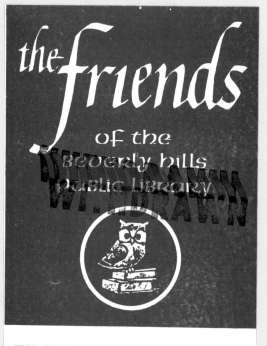

Bags and Purses
Vanda Foster

The Costume Accessories Series
General Editor: Dr Aileen Ribeiro

Distributed by

DRAMA BOOK PUBLISHERS

821 Broadway   New York, New York   10003

Acknowledgment

To all my good friends
from Platt Hall.

ISBN 0 7134 3772 3

Typeset by Tek-Art Ltd, London SE20
and printed in Great Britain by
Butler & Tanner Ltd
Frome, Somerset
for the publishers
B. T. Batsford Ltd
4 Fitzhardinge Street
London W1H 0AH

Vanda Foster is former keeper of the Gallery of English Costume, Manchester, and co-author of *Crinolines and Crimping Irons in Victorian Clothes: How they were Cleaned and Cared for*, published by Peter Owen, 1978.

I would like to thank the following for providing help and information during the preparation of this book. Miss Kay Staniland of the Museum of London; Miss Santina Levey and Mr Roger Pinkham of the Victoria and Albert Museum; Miss Jane Tozer of the Gallery of English Costume; Miss Janet Arnold; Mr Jeremy Farrell of the Museum of Costume, Nottingham; Miss Penny Byrde and Mrs M.E. Mines of the Museum of Costume, Bath; Miss Fiona Clarke of the Museum and Art Gallery, Worthing; Mrs Victoria Gabbitas of the Museum of Leathercraft, Northampton; Mrs Pat Clegg of the Castle Museum, York; Miss Anne Balfour-Paul of the Gunnersbury Park Museum, London; Mrs Stella Blum and Miss Jean Mailey of the Metropolitan Museum of Art, New York; Matthew X. Kiernan of the Museum of Fine Arts, Boston; Miss Elizabeth Ann Coleman of the Brooklyn Museum; Edward Maeder of the Los Angeles County Museum of Art; Mrs R. Andrews of Harrods; Mr R. Hardy of the Cordwainers Technical College; the John Lewis Partnership; Louis Vuitton International; Mr Clive Shilton; Miss Sarah Bowman; Dr Aileen Ribeiro.

Contents

List of Illustrations

Introduction

'The Splendid Shilling' mocks the pow'r of time,
And glows through ages in Miltonic verse,
But never poet, or in blank or rhyme,
Paid cheerful homage to an empty purse.

(*The Lady's Magazine*, 1799)

Men and women have used some sort of coin purse or container for as long as they have had money to carry, and at many stages of our history, they have kept this in a larger purse or bag, together with whatever personal belongings were necessary to the daily life of the time. Throughout history, bags have been used for a wide variety of purposes. As luggage they protect and transport goods, as dress bags they are storage containers, as visiting card purses or tobacco pouches, protective coverings for individual items. Some of the larger, more specialized bags of the Middle Ages played so important a part that their names are still current. A 'budget', for example, was a handbag for documents long before it was particularly associated with accounts. Similarly, the 'male' was often a travel bag, and it was only through its capacity as a container of letters, that it gave its name 'mail' to our letter post. Yet, despite their long and important usage, the history of bags and purses has rarely been considered, and little has been written about them.

In the case of the handbag, this is partly because the modern framed leather bag has been with us only since the second half of the nineteenth century, so that the present handbag trade has no great history. In the Middle Ages, stiffened leather bags belonged to the realms of the luggage makers, and the separate guilds of pouchmakers and pursers, who worked in soft leathers, merged with the fancy leather goods trade as early as the sixteenth century.

For much of their history, handbags and purses have been chameleon objects, changing their forms and materials radically according to the current tastes and demands. Unlike shoes or gloves, they are not limited by the need to fit part of the human anatomy, and can appear in almost any shape or size. Nor have they been restricted to one particular type of material. We may associate bags and purses with leather, and indeed, the durability, lightness, and suppleness of leather have made it a popular choice, but bags and purses have been made in almost every material known to man. In the seventeenth century, they were often made of silk embroidered with silver, gold and pearls; in the eighteenth century of glass beads, net, or woven grass; the Victorians delighted in purses of silver, enamels, ormolu, ivory or shell; while the twentieth century has seen them made of feathers, paper, wood and plastic.

This adaptability has made bags and purses particularly expressive of the needs and tastes of their time. With little restriction as to shape or material, they have been ideal vehicles for popular decorative techniques, both professional and amateur, and one can trace the history of embroidery and other decorative arts in the handbag.

As containers of the equipment of daily life, their forms have been strongly influenced by current developments in technology and social usage. Improvements in rail travel produced sturdy framed bags to carry personal necessities more securely on long journies, while the development of air travel counteracted this with the demand for light-weight materials. Women's emancipation brought the need to carry latch keys, car keys, cheque books, and business papers, as well as the ever-widening range of cosmetics, while trousers for women, and slimmer-fitting, lightweight clothes for men, have produced the modern unisex bags. The growth of cosmetics, the introduction of smoking, and changes from coinage to bank notes and credit cards, have all been reflected in the design of bags and purses.

Although all bags are closely linked, and there has been a constant interchange of style and usage between purses, handbags, luggage and other containers, I have tried to restrict this book to those containers for money and general daily necessities, which are carried on the person, for these are most closely related to fashions in dress and decorative arts, and are most evocative of the daily life of their times.

1
1600-1800

FROM POUCHES TO POCKETS

Before the sixteenth century, both men and women kept their valuables and personal belongings in bags or pouches attached to their girdles. Naturally, both the form and the contents of these bags varied according to fashion, and the status and lifestyle of the wearer, but among the wealthy they were often made of the richest silks and set on ornate metal frames, in a range of beautiful and inventive designs.

During the reign of Elizabeth I, however, fashionable dress became increasingly stiff and formal. Women's bodices and men's doublets were long-waisted and rigid, their sleeves full and padded. Men's breeches were filled out with interlinings of wool, horsehair, or even bran, while women's skirts were distended to enormous proportions by a variety of farthingales in the form of hooped petticoats or rolls of padding. Coin purses and other small items could easily be hidden in such voluminous clothing, so that girdle pouches became both impractical and unnecessary, and by the turn of the century they had disappeared from fashionable use.

In the seventeenth and eighteenth centuries the

---

1 Dutch engraving, 1600-1610. The women are being fitted with roll farthingales. The attendant on the left has an old-fashioned girdle pouch, while the fashionable woman on the right wears a tasselled purse with long drawstrings under her gown.

more elaborate versions survived only in the fossilized forms of ceremonial dress, or in specialized bags such as those used by huntsmen. A game bag in the Burrell collection, said to have been used by James I, together with matching gloves and falcon's hood, is embroidered in the pattern of coiling stems typical of its time, but its metal frame and flared shape are still in the style of the mediaeval girdle pouch.[1]

A smaller leather pouch also survived in the dress of the Scottish Highlander, whose narrow kilt made it essential, and when the kilt became established as a national costume, this 'sporran' remained a permanent feature. It was only as Highland dress became increasingly ceremonial that the sporran became more elaborate.

Apart from these exceptions, bags and pouches were used in the seventeenth century only by the elderly, like Shakespeare's 'slippered pantaloon, With spectacles on nose and pouch on side',[2] or by the poorer classes, for whom a large leather bag was essential to contain the basic necessities of life. Thus in 1688, the leather book bag or 'satchel' had become the 'Plow Man's Pantry, in which his provisions is put, and carried on his shoulder'.[3] In 1611 the 'budget'

held the pedlar's 'small wares',[4] while by 1698, the double-ended 'wallet' was used by the likes of the old blind pensioner who 'out of a wallet which had as many partitions as an old country cupboard, for his silver farthings, short pipes, tobacco, and bread and cheese etc. . . pulls out a couple of little flutes'.[5] By the early years of the seventeenth century, the expression 'to turn to bag and wallet' had come to imply a life of poverty and begging.[6]

In fashionable circles, the pouch was not so much replaced as moved. Men took advantage of their voluminous clothing to transfer the soft leather pouch from their belts to the inside of their breeches, in the form of large chamois leather pockets. In these they might keep purse, mirror, comb, keys, seals, tobacco box, and later, snuff box, while the watch

---

2 Woman's drawstring purse, German, 1604. Chamois leather, embroidered in green silk with flowers, the intial 'M', and the date 1604. A complex design consisting of a large pouch with seven smaller pouches attached, each with its own leather drawstrings finished with green silk tassels. (26 x 17cm.)

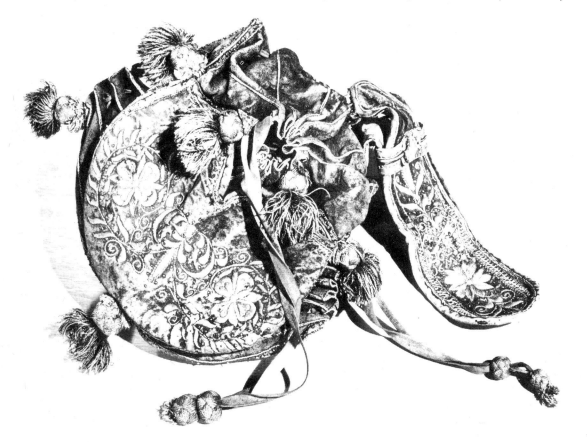

was held in a special fob pocket in the breeches waistband. A fine lace-edged handkerchief might be tucked into the slash of a padded sleeve, and a toothpick stuck in the hat, while muffs of silk or fur could also be used to contain small items. Even when the fashion for padding died out in the 1620s, breeches pockets were retained, and when in the 1660s the doublet was replaced by a long coat and waistcoat, these too were provided with deep slit pockets. Similarly, in the late eighteenth century, a fashion for a narrow silhouette, with tighter fitting breeches, still left pockets in the coat and waistcoat, while the watch and seals were hung from the waist on a decorative chain or chatelaine. It was only from the 1960s, when the fashion for slim-fitting coat and narrow trousers coincided with the discarding of the waistcoat, that men once again considered using bags instead of pockets.

Women, too, rejected the obvious use of the bag in the seventeenth century, preferring in many cases to hang long drawstring pouches underneath their huge skirts. In a Dutch engraving of about 1610, which shows women being fitted with the roll farthingales then used to pad the hips, the woman attendant still wears the old-style girdle pouch. The lady of fashion, on the other hand, raising her skirt to be fitted, reveals beneath it a tasselled drawstring bag hanging from her waist, over her petticoat. Naturally, such bags would never appear in the formal portraits of the period, but it may be that many of the little embroidered bags or purses which survive from the early seventeenth century were worn in this way, reached through the front opening of the skirt, or through slits in the side seams.

A popular alternative was to hang personal belongings from a girdle or clip at the waist. As yet, women carried little about them in the way of cosmetics, for most of their washes, pastes and pomatums were kept in pots and bottles, to be applied in the boudoir, but other fashionable accessories might include a fan, hand mirror, watch, needlework tools, and a sweet-smelling pomander, all of which could be suspended from the waist:

Nor here omit the bob of gold
Which a pomander ball does hold,
This to her side she does attach
With gold crochet, or French pennache[7]

The muff and hat were also used as handy containers, by women as by men.

Inset pockets were another alternative. According to the wardrobe inventories of Elizabeth I they were frequently used, at least in loose gowns, throughout the last quarter of the sixteenth century. They feat-ure too, in a skirt of the 1660s which survives in the Costume Museum at Bath[8], but they may not have been used much later than this, since they never appear in eighteenth-century gowns.

In that century, a fashionable alternative was a new version of the ornamental girdle, later to be named the chatelaine. This consisted of a decorative plaque which hooked on to the waistband, and from which was suspended a number of chains, each supporting some useful accessory such as a watch, a seal, a key, and perhaps a writing tablet, needlework tools, or a toothpick. The richest of these chatelaines were made of gold and precious stones, but more popular were silver, the yellow alloy 'pinchbeck', or cut steel, sometimes decorated with enamels or Wedgwood jasper-ware cameos. They were particularly popular from the 1770s, when it was fashionable for both men and women to wear two watches, or a watch and a miniature of a loved one, one suspended on each hip.

These chatelaines were expensive items, however, and most women preferred a cheaper and more practical means of carrying personal belongings — the tie pocket.

TIE POCKETS

> Lucy Locket lost her pocket,
> Kitty Fisher found it,
> Not a penny was there in it,
> Only ribbons round it.[9]

Lucy Locket and Kitty Fisher were well known in the mid-eighteenth century, the former as a character in *The Beggar's Opera*, and the latter as a noted courtesan, painted by Reynolds in 1759. The type of detachable pocket, bound with ribbon, was equally well known, and could well have been worn by either lady. It consisted of a flat fabric bag, closed at the top, but with an opening at the front, and was attached to a tape which tied around the waist, under the skirts. Many pockets were worn in pairs, one on each hip, and were reached through pocket holes in the sides of the gown.

Early examples may have been more like the drawstring pouch seen in the Dutch engraving. When Sir Ralph Verney was in France, in 1650, he sent the wife of the French ambassador a gift of 'an excellent Spanish pocket cover [sic] with Scarlet Taffety'.[10] Since the silk taffeta was only a covering, and Spain was then renowned for its soft leather goods, this may well have been a leather bag, not unlike the old-fashioned leather pouch.

Certainly, tie pockets seem to have been well known by the middle of the century, for Alice Morse

Earle, the American costume historian, found the entry 'a pair of pockets' in several colonial inventories of that time, and she also described a seventeenth-century print of Oliver Cromwell preaching, in which 'a pickpocket has raised the gown-skirt of a rapt woman listener, and is rifling her hanging-pocket'.[11] (Clearly, the position of the pocket was no deterrent to the would-be thief. Indeed, many were proud of the skill it demanded: 'My chief dexterity was in robbing the ladies. There is a peculiar delicacy required in whipping one's hand up a lady's petticoats and carrying off her pockets'.)[12]

Certainly in the eighteenth century, pockets were often found in pairs, attached to the same waist tape. Ranging from 20cm to 30cm in length, they could be drop- or pear-shaped, or almost triangular. The central slit was generally vertical, although some examples have a curved horizontal aperture, to fit the hand, and both slit and edges are usually bound with silk ribbon or linen tape.

Although some were made of printed calicoes, most were embroidered, the embroidery having been worked in pocket shape before the fabric was cut out. Silk, linen and cotton were all used, but the most popular fabric was white dimity, a sturdy linen and cotton twill, which was further strengthened with a lining of buckram or canvas. A favourite type of embroidery was a trail of exotic flowers in brightly

coloured worsteds, but alternatives included flame-stitch, petit point, whitework, or patchwork. Many a young girl practised her embroidery in 'working a pocket' for herself or a friend, and some are signed or dated.

They could also be bought ready-made. In 1769, a London haberdasher advertised pockets of dimity or fustian (another type of mixed linen and cotton fabric), while Boilieu and Paradine, the Whitechapel milliners, stocked ready-made 'Dimitty and Ticking pockets'[13] as well as the fabrics for making them up. Surviving examples include a range of pockets worked in yellow silk in vermicular lines of quilting, a favourite professional technique.

Styles of dress influenced the way in which the pocket was worn. In the 1650s, when the skirt of the gown was only slightly parted in front to reveal the decorative petticoat, the pocket may have been worn just under the skirt, but the fashion for looping back the gown, which appeared in the 1680s, revealed

3 *Woman's tie pocket, 1774. White corded linen embroidered in brightly coloured worsteds, mainly in chain stitch, the slits and edges bound with pink wool braid. Worn round the waist, under the skirts. (The eyelet holes in the waist tapes are an unusual feature, probably indicating later use.) (Height 42cm.)*

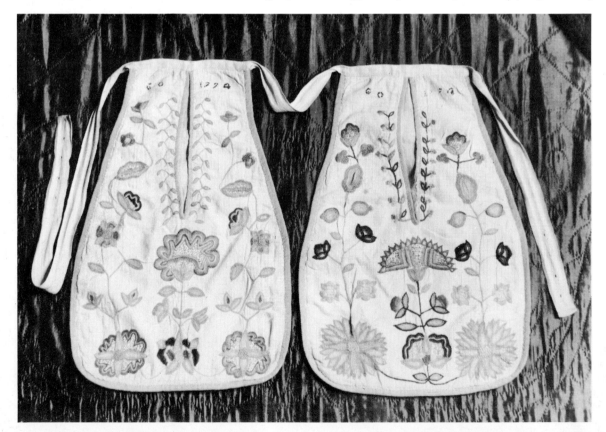

4 Caricature of Mrs Siddons by Gillray, 1784. She wears tie pockets under her gown, but over her petticoat, and is reaching for a netted wallet purse.

same position. This may be artistic licence, since the pockets full of money were crucial to Gillray's satire on her alleged greed, but it is likely that this more convenient position was popular for informal wear, even among the fashionable.

In these sturdy, capacious pockets, women kept all their basic necessities, including loose coins, a purse, or a pocket book, together with a 'pincase, wipe and bunch of keys'.[14] One eighteenth-century New Englander bequeathed her pocket to a lifelong friend, together with its contents of a mirror, hand warmer, and, still more warming, 'a strong-waters bottle'.[15] At a time when gin and spirits were cheap, a flask was often carried, and Humphrey Clinker's Aunt Tabitha revived the half-conscious Matt Bramble with just such 'a mouthful of cordial, which she always keeps in her pocket'.[16]

5 Gentleman with purse, late 16th century. This type of soft drawstring purse was popular throughout the 17th and 18th centuries.

so much of the petticoat that, from this time at least, the pocket was worn underneath it. Thus pocket holes were introduced into the petticoat itself, and were often trimmed with embroidery or fancy braid, as a decorative feature in their own right. After 1710, for all but Court dress, skirt drapery went out of fashion, and the skirt hung loose. With this style, pocket holes became no more than discreet slits in the gown, and open side seams in the petticoat. Even with the wide, oblong hoops of the 1740s, access to pockets was maintained, for although both gown and petticoat were extended at the sides, the top edges were left open above matching slits in the hooped petticoat itself.

In the last quarter of the century, contemporary engravings often show women of the poorer classes wearing their pockets over their petticoats, within easy reach of the front opening of the gown, but generally hidden by a large apron. Gillray's caricature of Mrs Siddons as Melpomene shows them in the

SEVENTEENTH-CENTURY SWEET BAGS AND PURSES

Despite the introduction of pockets, frequent use was made by both sexes of a small bag or purse in which to carry loose coins. These are rarely depicted in portraits or prints, but mention is made of them in contemporary writings.

Many were made of leather, like that bought for a penny by Lord Howard of Naworth in 1629.[17] Others were made of knitted wool or silk, or woven silk, usually in a simple rectangular form, but always closed with long tasselled drawstrings. Purse frames seem to have gone out of fashion in the seventeenth century. Dr Cunnington quotes a reference of 1607 to 'a leather Pouch with a Snap-haunce shut', but this was undoubtedly an old girdle pouch, since the wearer was a down-at-heel 'country-fellow', whose outfit 'was not worth twelve-pence'.[18] The few examples of metal frames which survive from the seventeenth century are on large bags used either for hunting or for ceremonial purposes, which in both cases were based on earlier styles. They do not seem to have been used for small purses.

The drawstrings were sometimes used to hang the

6 *French gaming purse, c.1630, detail from a painting by A. Baugin. Gaming purses had flat circular bases and high pleated sides which contained the coins or counters as in a dish. They were closed by plaited drawstrings and pulled open by means of the silk covered toggles.*

purse from the belt, when it became easy prey for the 'nip' or 'cutpurse'. Robert Greene, in his treatise on thievery and 'cony-catching' in 1591, vividly described the art of this thief with his special knife or 'cuttle', which could slice through the strings, or even the body of the purse itself, with such ease that one poor victim 'suspected nothing till he had sold a peck of meal, and offered for to change money, and then he found his purse bottomless'.[19]

The fashion for long purse-strings was retained even when the purse was tucked in a sleeve or pocket: 'For his purse . . . lay in the sleeve of his doublet . . . . A fair new purse with white strings and great tassels . . . thrust it into the slop of his hose, as he was wont, letting the strings thereof hang out for a traine'.[20] In these circumstances the strings might be put to more practical use, and Greene describes a purse 'at the one string whereof was fastened a little key, and at the other his signet ring'.[21]

Before the age of standard bank bills and cheque books, the coins carried in such purses might amount to considerable sums. A pickpocket described by Greene 'foisted' a purse containing 'seven pound in gold, beside thirty shillings and odd white money',[22] while that of a rich farmer, up from the country, might contain twenty or thirty pounds. On the other hand, the purse of a young blood fresh from the gaming table might reveal 'nothing therein but white counters, a thimble and a broken threepence'.[23]

Gaming was a fashionable pastime during the seventeenth century. Elizabeth I was fond of cards, and at Stuart Courts thousands of pounds were lost and won at dice and card games like Ombre, Quadrille, Basset and Trolle Madam. According to *The Compleat Gamester* of 1674, anyone who appeared ignorant of the game in vogue would be reckoned 'low-bred and hardly fit for conversation'.

Players kept the requisite money or counters in special gaming purses designed for the purpose. These were drawstring bags, but with stiffened circular bases which sat flat upon the table, and stiffened pleated sides which contained the coins as in a dish. Purses in this style appear on gaming prints of the seventeenth century, and are embroidered into trompe l'oeil designs on card tables of the time of Queen Anne. A number of surviving examples are made of white kid, covered in velvet, and encrusted in metal thread embroidery. Stylized motifs, including fleurs de lis, are worked down the pleated sides, and the bases show coats of arms, presumably to identify each gamester's 'chips'. Some examples are quite small, but the largest of those at the Victoria and Albert Museum has a base more than 12cm in diameter, and is 11cm deep. Although probably of French manufacture, purses like these were used in England and other parts of Europe. In some cases the leather was perfumed:

> To play at ombre, or basset,
> She a rich pulvil purse must get,
> With guineas fill'd, on cards to lay,
> With which she fancies most to play.[24]

(*Pulvil* was the Portugese term for powders and perfume.)

Although expensive and elaborate purses were in practical daily use among the rich, most of those which survive in museums probably owe their preservation to the fact that they have obviously never been carried on a regular basis. The seventeenth-century purse had a variety of functions and the finest examples may well have been novelties, souvenirs, or elaborate packaging for a gift of perfume or money.

There are numerous references among the New Year's gift lists of Elizabeth I, and in seventeenth-century family records, to items described as 'sweet bags', which appear to have contained scented herbs or essences. Before the widespread use of adequate drainage and washing facilities, evil smells were an accepted part of life, but if they could not be avoided,

they could at least be disguised, by the use of pomanders and perfumes. The accounts of the Earl of Bedford in the 1680s show that he spent considerable sums on scented powder for his linen, hair and hands, on Queen of Hungary's water and orange flower water, to be used as an after-shave, and on other essences and perfume balls. He also bought scented powder to put into 'sweet bags'. Made of sarsenet, a light silk taffeta, these were sometimes bought ready-made, and sometimes made up by his housekeeper.[25]

Other references suggest that sweet bags were more than just herbal sachets, however, and that the term may have been extended to describe a decorative purse in which the sachets were placed. Certainly, sweet bags were often very elaborately embroidered, as can be seen from a selection of those listed in the

---

7 *Gaming purses, French, late 16th/early 17th century. Made of white kid covered with silk velvet and embroidered with metal threads. Plaited metal drawstrings and tassels. The owner's coat of arms was often embroidered on the base to ensure correct identification of the winnings. (Left purse 13cm diameter.)*

inventory of Henry Howard, Earl of Northampton, in 1614:

- one large cloth of silver sweet bagge embroidered with pinched plate of golde lined with russet Taffeta
- a smaller sweet bagge embroidered with high embosted mosseworke havinge two sea nymphs upon dolphins and other figures of fowles, edged about with lace of silver and gold, lined with carnation
- a small white satten sweet bagge embroidered with flies, wormes, and flowers in silke and golde
- one small sweet bag of Tent work, the ground silver with pottes and flowers lined with green sattin[26]

Similarly, in 1639, Lady Sussex asked Sir Ralph Verney to purchase trimmings for a 'swite bag' which, from her description, was to be quite an elaborate affair. It included lace with silver thread and spangles, six yards of silk ribbon for the strings and some edging lace 'as slite as may bee to ege the stringes and but littill silver in it; ten yardes will be enofe'.[27] The length of the strings suggests that it was quite large, and it may well have been intended as a scented container for clothing, perhaps even dirty clothing, if we are to judge by Evelyn's description of a lady's dressing room of 1690, which contained 'two high embroidered sweet bags', used 'to put up rags'.[28]

Smaller versions may actually have been worn on the person. Certainly both men and women carried scented handkerchiefs and 'sweet gloves' rubbed with perfumed oils, so that it is quite probable that they should carry a 'sweet bag' or purse containing a scented sachet.

A group of bags survive in museums whose decoration corresponds very closely to those in the Northampton inventory, particularly that described as 'tent work'. These exquisite little bags are all about 10cm to 13cm square. They can be made of silk, leather or velvet, but the majority are of linen canvas embroidered all over with coloured silks in tent stitch, with dense patterns of plants, animals and insects. The most usual design is that of intertwining stems, branching from a central trunk, or coiling in symmetrical patterns like an embroidered knot garden. The plants depicted are those favourites of the Elizabethan gardener, the rose, honeysuckle, cornflower, viola and pink, together with bunches of grapes, wild strawberries, and the bursting peapod, then still a novelty on English soil. Among these plants, the embroiderer might set butterflies, caterpillars, birds or beasts, which are quite out of proportion, but whose stylized forms blend easily into the overall pattern.

Such embroideries are typical of Elizabethan and early Stuart work, and can be found on many other costume accessories (although they were rarely made to match, each item being valued rather as a work of craftsmanship in its own right).

Taking her patterns from printed sources such as herbals and bestiaries, and perhaps making use of a professional pattern drawer, the amateur needlewoman could produce work of the highest quality. Many of these little bags, however, have the stamp of the professional embroiderer, working for the luxury trade. Patterns are standardized and there is considerable use of metal threads and complex stitches. Some show silver thread worked in gobelin stitch to give a solid silver ground, like Northampton's 'cloth of silver'. Others used padded metal threads, seed pearls, or raised work stitches to give three-dimensional effects, or 'embosted worke'.

Lined with richly coloured silk taffetas, they are closed by drawstrings of plaited silk and metal threads. The twisting of these cords was an art in itself, and was done by hand, using a small lyre-shaped implement called a lucette. Pattern books were issued in the early seventeenth century devoted entirely to the plaiting of braids and purse strings, and some intricate designs used as many as twelve strands.

Further trimmings include wooden knobs on each drawstring, delicately worked in silk threads; three tassels on the base of the bag; and, for pulling the bag open, two large knots made of loops of silver wire, interwoven in openwork patterns. Some bags have the addition of a tiny matching pincushion, which again suggests that these were made for women to carry or have about them.

The majority of these bags or purses, with their coiling stem and flower designs, belong to the early years of the century. A number with obelisk patterns are probably of the time of James I, when such architectural motifs seem to have been particularly popular, but a few were still being made in the last quarter

---

8 Purses or sweet bags, early 17th century. The square purses are of canvas lined with silk and embroidered with metal thread grounds. The flowers are worked in coloured silks in tent stitch (except for bottom right, which is worked in chain stitch with raised work petals in buttonhole stitch). Top left has a matching pincushion. Middle right is in the form of a bunch of grapes in silk and metal threads, padded and worked in buttonhole stitch. (Square purses approx. 12cm square.)

9 Drawstring purses, 17th century. Top left, *frog purse of cream silk embroidered with silver thread. His mouth forms the opening.* Top right, *nut purse, each half separately covered with silk and linked by silk gussets. Embroidered in silks, silver threads, seed pearls and coral beads. (Width 3cm.)* Bottom, *ribbon purse of pale blue silk woven with silver thread, decorated with applied silver lace, and edged with bright orange silk ribbon loops, 1660-80.*

of the century, and these show a very different style of embroidery. Worked in rococo stitch on linen canvas, the most usual design is an all-over diaper pattern, and the only remnant of the naturalistic Elizabethan flowers is in tiny geometric flower heads or strawberries, forming a spot in the centre of each square. Two bags in the Metropolitan Museum of New York which have larger, more detailed flowers, but arranged in a regular repeat pattern, show the intermediate stage.

Apart from these square embroidered sweet bags, or purses, there is also a group of tiny novelties which may have been used either as coin purses or as perfume sachets. One example in the Victoria and Albert Museum is in the form of a bunch of grapes. Made of silk, embroidered in blue and green silks, and highlighted with metal thread, each individual 'grape' is separately padded and worked in buttonhole stitch, while the top is finished off with a stylized silk vine leaf. Closed by plaited drawstrings of pink and silver thread, and lined with pink and silver tissue, the whole bag is only 7.5cm long.

In 1609, a character in one of Ben Jonson's Masques conjured with the idea of making a 'purset' from the skin of a frog, and the same inspiration lies behind a tiny purse at the Museum of London.[29] Made of cream silk, worked with a mesh of silver thread, it is in the shape of a frog, whose mouth forms the opening.

Even more remarkable are a group of little bags each of which is made from an open nut. Each half is covered with silk and linked to the other by a silk gusset. Some are embroidered with circles of couched silk and metal thread around a minute bead, and they fasten by a plaited drawstring slotted through the gusset. When closed they are no more than 3cm wide.

These tiny novelties could have contained no more than a single coin or a few scented herbs, and their impracticality and lavish decoration suggest that, like many seventeenth-century bags, their prime function was as a luxurious gift.

'THE GIFT OF A FRIEND'

The costly materials and fine workmanship found in so many seventeenth-century bags and purses made them ideal gifts among the well-to-do. Embroidered bags and sweet bags appear regularly in the lists of New Year gifts presented to Elizabeth I, as do sums of money in purses of knitted or woven silk. By the late sixteenth century the exchange of New Year's gifts had become an elaborate ritual by which the Crown was able to acquire goods of greater value than those which it gave out, and the amount each nobleman was expected to give was strictly laid down according to rank, together with the means of giving. Thus Henry, 5th Earl of Huntingdon, records that for New Year's Day 1604-5 he was expected to present King James with twenty pieces of gold, to the value of £20, for which he must buy a new purse worth about 5 shillings (receiving only 18oz of gilt plate in return).[30] In this case the purse was not only valuable in itself, but provided an elaborate gift packaging which helped to disguise the mercenary nature of the

transaction.

Royal visits were another occasion when full purses were presented to the monarch. When James I visited York in 1617 he received a standing cup and a purse of £3 value, containing one hundred double sovereigns. Four years earlier the mayor of Bristol had presented Queen Anne of Denmark with 'a fair purse of sattin, embroidered with the two letters A.R. for her name' and containing £110 in gold coins.[32]

Purses were also given as presents in their own right, however, as witnessed by a letter from Sir John Harington in 1602: 'My Lady Ambassador of France was entertained by the Queen yesterday very graciously, and gave among the Queen's maids French purses, fans and masks, very bountifully.'[33]

A group of beaded purses from the years 1620-40 appear to have been made primarily as gifts. These are flat leather drawstring bags about 13cm square, covered with coloured glass beads strung on a mesh of dark brown silk. The beads are usually arranged in diaper patterns or to form a design of acorns (perhaps as an incentive to save, on the grounds that 'great oaks from little acorns grow'). The upper part is often worked with the date and a simple motto such as 'Remember The Pore', 'Here it is Hit or Miss', or even 'The Gift of a Friend'.

Another more specialized type of gift purse was popular right at the end of the century. To a rich silk drawstring bag were bound two enamelled metal plaques, each painted with a portrait — a man on one side and woman on the other — dressed in the fashions of the 1690s. These were a speciality of the French town of Limoges, long famous for its enamels, and are said to have been marriage purses, presented by the groom to the bride during the ceremony, as a symbol of his endowment of worldly goods. The portraits represented the happy couple.

Even in the seventeenth century, France dominated the market in luxury goods and accessories, and many gift purses seem to have been French made, particularly those obviously intended as marriage purses or lovers' gifts. A large number dating from around the end of the century are made of tapestry woven silk, brocaded and embroidered with flaming hearts, cupids, and lovers' mottoes, and made up into drawstring purses consisting of four shield-shaped panels bound with metal braid. One fine example in the Metropolitan Musuem is woven entirely in silver thread, and is embroidered in black and silver-gilt with designs of cupids, butterflies, hearts and scrolls, and the inscriptions *Au plus fidel* (to the most faithful), *Voilà mon tresor* (here is my treasure), *Je fuit la fou(le)* (I fly from the crowd), and *Rien ne m'arrête*

(nothing stops me).

A flat drawstring purse, almost semi-circular in shape, was popular after the middle of the century. One of light blue silk, in the Museum of London, is edged with loops of ribbon in salmon pink silk, just like those used to trim coats, breeches and gloves in the 1660s: 'It was a fine silken thing which I spied walking the other day . . . that had as much ribbon about him as would have plundered six shops . . . and the colours were Red, Orange, and Blew, of well gum'd sattin'.[34] Although made of expensive materials, the body of the purse is decorated simply with applied bands of silver lace. The delicate craftsmanship and rich imaginative designs of Elizabethan and early Jacobean embroideries had disappeared by the second half of the century, particularly in professional work.

By the last quarter of the century, the drawstring purse made of four shield-shaped panels was the most popular style. Even Lord and Lady Clapham, the two dolls of the 1690s at the Victoria and Albert Museum, have amongst their accessories a purse of this type. Theirs is made of brocaded silk, the base and drawstrings trimmed with silver thread buttons, but tapestry woven silk was the most usual fabric, brocaded and embroidered with tiny stylized figures and flowers. One example at the Castle Museum, York, has two sides worked with coats of arms, perhaps to commemorate a marriage, while the other two sides show the ever popular flower sprigs and a stag. Other examples display the same preoccupation with the exotic that influenced all forms of decoration at this period. Some include the figures of blackamoors, while one in Boston depicts the four corners of the globe, as symbolized by female figures and exotic animals.

A distinctive feature of these purses is their elaborate tassels made of heavy bunches of silk and metal threads. Decorative tassels appeared on purses throughout the seventeenth century, inspiring one botanist in 1629 with the useful comparison, 'The whole stalke with the flowers upon it doth somewhat resemble a long Purse tassel'.[35] By the end of the century, however, they were particularly large and

bushy, reflecting an interest in techniques of knotting which can be found in other aspects of purses at this time.

Knotting was becoming a fashionable pastime in the late seventeenth century, probably imported from China, and many purses of this period are simple bags knotted in silk or metal mesh, and finished with tassels. Others were made by working the threads in a buttonhole technique, itself the beginnings of needlepoint lace. This was done on a special purse or thimble mould, in the form of a hollow tube of wood with a curved base and rows of holes at the top. Bands of thread were wound round the top of the mould, and secured by stitches passing through the holes. These bands formed the rim of the purse, from which rows of buttonhole stitches were worked to form the main body. Once these had been finished off at the base, the securing stitches were cut, and the purse released, ready to be trimmed with drawstrings and tassels.

Many patterns were worked in regular horizontal stripes, but using graduated colours, and favourite motifs were lines of strawberries in shaded pinks. More sophisticated designs included the popular hearts and cupids.

EIGHTEENTH-CENTURY PURSES

Purses continued to be valued as gifts throughout the eighteenth century, and the import of French purses with hearts and lovers' mottoes carried on for a number of years, while others were still used as containers for gifts of money. As late as 1771, Mrs Jenkins in *Humphrey Clinker* was presented with 'an Indian purse, made of silk grass, containing twenty crown pieces'.[36] The growing fashion for sentiment, however, combined with the popularity of home needlework, produced a vogue among women for presenting home-made purses to favoured gentlemen. William Cowper was inspired to write a poem to his cousin Anne Bodham, 'on receiving from her a network purse made by herself'[37], and by the late eighteenth century the giving of purses was so common that Lord Bessborough was forced to turn down such a gift from Sarah Ponsonby, saying 'I desire the favour of you not to send me the Purse you mention, for I have, I believe, twenty by me which are not of any use. It has been the fashion of ladies to make purses and they have been so obliging as to give me a great many'.[38] No wonder that so many survive apparently unused!

Gaming was as much a feature of life in the eighteenth century as in the seventeenth, and games like Loo, Whist and Quadrille were played by everyone

---

10 *Limoges enamel marriage purse, late 17th century. A bag of white silk and silver thread, sandwiched between two enamelled plaques. Silk cord drawstrings. Trimmings of red corded silk ribbon and silver fringe. The enamelled plaques show portraits of the bride and groom, and were a speciality of Limoges. (11.5 x 8cm.)*

from the Prince of Wales to the quiet country parson. Circular gaming purses, like those of the seventeenth century, appear on decorated card tables of the time of Queen Anne, and in 1751 Diderot's list of the

apprentice pieces made by a French pursemaker included a velvet-covered leather 'counter purse' in the same style.[39] By the 1780s, however, Rowlandson's prints show gamesters, both fashionable and unfashionable, with the ubiquitous wallet purse. The style of most eighteenth-century purses was governed by current fashion in decoration and needlework techniques, rather than by function.

A number of framed purses with catch fastenings survive from the first half of the century, many using a newly invented zinc and copper alloy, which imitated gold. In England this was called 'pinchbeck',

11 *Drawstring purse, late 17th century. Four-sided purse of tapestry woven silk and metal threads worked with two coats of arms, flower sprigs and a stag. The elaborate tassels are made of knotted metal threads. Possibly a marriage purse. (Each panel 7 x 8.5cm.)*

after its inventor Christopher Pinchbeck, but similar alloys were developed in France and Holland, at about the same time, and sold under different names.

There seem to have been two main types of frame. One was heavy and rectangular with a hooked catch, but no release mechanism, so that the two halves of the frame has to be prized apart. Because of its long sides, or 'legs', this type of frame opened very wide, and broad gussets had to be added at the sides, making this a very roomy style. The other type was flat and pear-shaped, with a more delicate curved frame. This also fastened with a hooked catch, but this could be released by pressing a central button on the other half of the frame.

Both types were embroidered according to current fashions. Some were made of silk worked with scrolling designs in padded metal strips and threads, others were of linen embroidered in wool, silk or metal often in tent stitch. Typical of the latter style

is a French purse at the Victoria and Albert Museum. Set on a rectangular pinchbeck frame, its shield-shaped panels are made of linen embroidered with silk and metal threads in laid and couched work and French knots. On one side is the figure of a huntsman with a wild boar, and on the other, Diana as huntress, dressed in contemporary style, her earrings and sleeve clasps picked out with raised metal threads.

Diderot's pursemaker, in 1751, made morocco leather purses with rectangular frames of iron or steel, as well as a hunting bag on a curved press-button frame, while in England, Coles Child the toy-man was advertising 'spring purses' (i.e. with a spring fastening) in 1755.[40]

Drawstring purses maintained their popularity, however. Of those that were professionally made some of the finest were the French *sablé* beaded purses which flourished in the middle half of the century. These made use of beads so minute that one might find as many as one thousand to the square inch, hence the term sablé (French for 'laid or covered with sand') which has long been used to describe this type of work.

The beads were strung on silk thread in horizontal rows (carefully arranged according to the overall design) and these rows were then mounted on a framework, to be linked together by simple looping stitches. Although considerable skill was required to

---

12 Wooden purse stretcher and moulds — for wallet purses. A wooden stretcher for netted wallet purses, used to pull out the mesh before the ends were sewn up. Left, a moule turc on which the stitches were formed round the pegs at the top. Right, a thimble mould — on which the purse was worked in button-hole stitch.

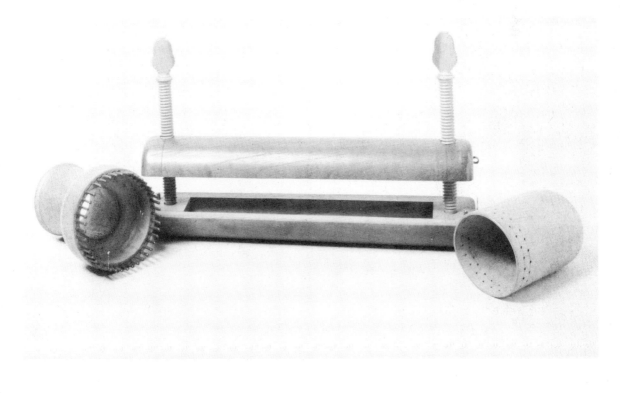

build up any form of pictorial design, many pieces show quite sophisticated scenes and portraits. The technique was used for a whole range of trinkets and accessories including book covers, boxes, chatelaines and shoes, and Larry Salmon, in his study of the unique collection at Boston Museum, has concluded that they were the work of one or two specialist Parisian workshops, and intended as 'playthings for the wealthiest classes in France'.[41]

Most of these purses are similar in construction, consisting of four wedge-shaped panels through which pass two drawstrings of plaited silk, finished with large wooden acorns covered with a net of sablé beads. Many show designs of coats of arms, or exotic flowers, in a range of delicate colours, but a number

show scenes of ballooning, and can thus be dated to the 1780s.

The first successful flight in a hot air balloon took place from the Bois de Boulogne on 21 November 1783, manned by Jean François Pilâtre de Rozier, and the Marquis d'Arlandes. It inspired a host of imitators on both sides of the Channel, and representations of balloons and their navigators appeared in contemporary prints and textiles, and produced such fashions as the 'balloon' hat. A sablé drawstring purse in the Boston collection features a portrait of Pilâtre de Rozier, taken from a contemporary print, together with a picture of a two-manned balloon. As a topical novelty it must have been made soon after the flight itself.

The English also produced commemorative souvenir purses, but, on the whole, the emphasis was on novelty rather than luxury. The Costume Museum at Nottingham has a rare example. Made of two panels of cream satin, lined with white silk and trimmed with green silk ribbons and rosettes, it is printed on both sides with a medallion containing the head of George III, and the date 'April 23, 1789'.

In the autumn of 1788, George III had suffered

---

13 Commemorative beadwork purse, French, 1783-4. Four triangular panels of multicoloured sablé beadwork, lined with pink silk. Plaited silk drawstrings with beaded acorn tassels. Shows a portrait of the balloonist Pilâtre de Rozier and the two-manned balloon in which he made his pioneer flight in 1783. (10.2 x 6.3cm.)

an illness so severe that the Whigs had campaigned for his abdication in favour of the Prince Regent. The King's sudden and unexpected recovery in the following February demanded a show of loyalty on all sides, and at the March Drawing Room all the ladies of the Court wore bandeaux embroidered 'God Save the King'. On 23 April, the King went in state to St Paul's Cathedral for a special thanksgiving service, and souvenir purses like this one were sold in the City of London to mark the occasion.

As a cheap and speedy method of production, printing was ideal for such novelties, and the delicacy of the printed line against the white background was also entirely suited to late eighteenth-century taste. The 1780s saw a marked preference for pale colours, light fabrics and small dainty patterns. Dresses were made of thin silks, light printed cottons, or white muslin, and fashionable embroideries on dresses and bags took the form of tiny flower sprigs, Neo-Classical medallions, and ribbon bows, worked in trailing lines of chain stitch or tambour.

Among amateur needlewomen, there was a vogue for openwork techniques like netting and knotting, and the result was a boom in home-made purses using these methods. Simple tubular drawstring purses netted in silk were sometimes interwoven with narrow silk ribbons, or lined with coloured silk to show off the mesh. Some were made of a thin bast fibre, rather like raffia, dyed in various colours and finished with loops of fibre in the form of bushy tassels. (Perhaps this was the 'silk grass' of Mrs Jenkins' Indian purse.) Others were made of fine net embroidered in stripes with sprigs of leaves and flowers, like 'the Rose-bud and sundry other Fancy Sprigs and Stripes' which could be made from the 'New-Invented Twist' advertised by one supplier in the 1780s.[42]

One of the most popular types of purse to emerge in the last quarter of the century, however, was the long tubular wallet purse, later known as a 'miser', 'ring' or 'stocking' purse. This consisted of a tube of fabric closed at each end, with a horizontal slit in the middle of one side. The contents were put through the slit and allowed to fall into either end of the tube, which was then picked up and carried by the middle. Two silver or cut steel rings, or 'sliders',

14 *Commemorative printed purse, 1789. Two panels of white satin printed in brown with the head of George III and the date 23 April 1789. Green silk piping, ribbons and bows. Made to commemorate the King's recovery from a long illness and sold on the day of his thanksgiving service. (20 x 11cm.)*

were fitted around the middle and could then be slid down towards the ends to gather the fabric together and so enclose the contents. This purse obviously derived from the early type of double-ended wallet used by countrymen and beggars.

Some early examples were in fact one-ended, and with their rounded base, pointed top, and high-set opening, were very similar in shape to hanging pockets. One in the Victoria and Albert Museum has the main body worked on a purse-mould with a design of strawberries, while the pointed top is in a simple green netted mesh. Sometimes a single slider was used to close off the contents at the bottom.

The double-ended version was the most popular, however, and in this form was still being made for gaming counters in the 1920s. Those of the late eighteenth century were particularly large, up to 44cm in length, and were often tucked in the belt. Although many were knitted or purse-moulded, the favourite technique with the amateur needlewoman was netting, and Catherine Hutton, recalling her life at this time, claimed 'to have netted upwards of a hundred wallet purses'.[43] The appropriate purse silk or 'twist' could be bought from specialist shops such as that of Thomas Gardom, the purse and watch chain maker of St James's Street, who advertised that 'Ladies may be accommodated with great Choice of Purse-Twist, Tassels and Sliders of all Sorts . . . . Ladies own work neatly dressed and made up; also every other Article in the Netting branch'.[44] The favourite colour seems to have been green, the traditional colour of love, for many of these purses were made by young ladies for their admirers. (Early in the next century, Thackeray's Becky Sharp was to advertise her devotion and capabilities to Joseph Sedley by netting him a green silk purse.)[45]

THE PURSE TRADE

Many purses of the seventeenth and eighteenth centuries were the work of professional pursemakers and could be bought ready made, although some gift and marriage purses must have been specially commissioned. Even those labours of love produced by amateur needlewomen were often taken to a professional to be made up and trimmed, and in 1624 Lord Howard of Naworth paid 2 shillings for 'trimming a purse for my lady'. In 1618 he paid one Mr

Gray no less than 13 shillings 4 pence for 'making up' two purses, the expense of which may imply that they were made from scratch rather than finished with costly trimmings.[46]

By this time, however, pursemaking was no longer regarded as a major trade in its own right, In mediaeval London, there had been separate craft guilds for pouchmakers and pursers, but the latter ceded to the more powerful glovers in 1498. Similarly, in the early sixteenth century, both glovers and pouchmakers merged with the leathersellers, who dominated the trade in soft leather goods, and from then on, pursemaking in England remained under the umbrella of the fancy goods trade.

This was not the case in Europe. In Germany, where mediaeval styles continued longer in use, the Nuremburg pouchmakers were still a separate and flourishing profession in the early seventeenth century. In France, too, where the importance of the silk industry served to promote all the related fashion trades, pursemaking remained an important craft in its own right. Diderot's *Encyclopédie* of 1751 included a section on the *Boursier* who was known chiefly for his purses, although he also made leather breeches, silk wig bags, caps and silk umbrellas. His wide range of fashionable goods included hunting bags and book bags as well as framed purses of morocco leather, knitted money purses, and drawstring purses of velvet, embroidered with silver and gold.

In eighteenth-century England, pursemakers were rarely mentioned as such, and certainly towards the end of the century those who did advertise usually claimed another primary trade. James Turner of Bloomsbury who made 'the very finest Silk Net Work, long and short Purses' called himself a 'Watch String and Purse Maker' and stocked a whole range of silk threads, metal beads and other goods.[47]

In fact purses could be bought from a wide range of shops selling fancy goods or trimmings. Stockists of dress trimmings and accessories, such as milliners and haberdashers, usually sold silk purses and 'purse-twist', and in 1793 Parson Woodforde bought a silk purse for 2 shillings from Reeves Hosiery Warehouse in the Strand.[48] At John Moggridge, the London cutler, one might find not only small metal buttons, clasps, and fittings, but knotting shuttles and work bags, gaming counters and backgammon tables, as well as 'Silk, Silver and Gold Purses'.[49] Toy makers, then dealers in trinkets rather than children's playthings, stocked a similar range, as did hardwaremen, while perfumers sold all sorts of scented leather goods, pocket books, cases, purses and bags. In 1794 Bettisons, the perfumers of Bloomsbury and Margate,

advertised silk purses, 'balloon purses, single and double' in gold and silver, and 'Lock and Tuck' purses, probably made of leather.[50]

For those with little access to towns and shops, small goods like purses could also be bought at fairs, or from pedlars. Many a traditional pedlar doll from the late eighteenth and early nineteenth centuries carries a miniature wallet purse among her wares.

LETTER CASES AND POCKET BOOKS

While purses were ideal for carrying coins and small trinkets, a larger, flatter container was necessary to safeguard precious letters, papers and bank bills, and a good number of these 'letter cases' survive from the seventeenth century. Rarely more than 16cm wide or 11cm high when closed, they are usually envelope-shaped and made in a variety of rich materials. Some are of French silk, tapestry woven in elaborate designs of hunting scenes or figures from La Fontaine's fables, while examples in French beadwork or Italian knitted silk survive from the very end of the century.

An English case, which once belonged to Admiral Sir William Penn, is in the double form with two pockets one above the other, which fold together under the envelope flap. Made of silk, it is embroidered on one side with Penn's coat of arms, and on the reverse the initials WP above the figure of a man in the dress of the 1650s. He is examining an astronomical globe, and beside him lies his faithful dog, the word 'PORT' written on its collar. The scene probably records Penn's great victory over the Spaniards at Port Elizabeth, Jamaica, in 1655, the case having been made as a gift to commemorate that event.[51]

A later example, now in the Museum of Leathercraft, is associated with the diarist Samuel Pepys. Made of brown morocco, it is embroidered in silver wire with a design of scrolling flowers and on one side the name 'Sam! Pepys Esq' and on the other the words 'Constantinople 1687'. Unfortunately, there is no record of Pepys having visited Constantinople in that year, but in his influential position as Secretary of the Admiralty, this case may well have been a gift from a Turkish envoy.

(Constantinople seems to have been well known for these decorative cases. The Costume Museum at Nottingham has a similar one dated 1717, while the Museum of Fine Arts at Boston has one of lavishly embroidered silk marked 'Constantinople 1755'.)

Another range of flat cases with attached note books were obviously intended to be carried on the person, since they were christened 'pocket books'. In Fielding's *Tom Jones* Sophia Western kept one, and inscribed her name on the first page[52], while Smollett's Roderick Random wrote names and addresses in his.[53] Women were renowned for making great use of these little books, as witnessed by a poem published in the *Gentleman's Magazine* of 1753, which listed among the typical contents 'scandal, dress or china ware . . . . A list of lovers, or of rhymes, Or pug's disease, or Betty's crimes' together with 'tea table heads' (headdresses), 'crippl'd verse', and 'silken shreds' (probably samples of dress fabrics).

Publishers were quick to realize the potential of

16 *Letter case or pocket book, 1687. Brown goat-skin (morocco) embroidered with silver wire. A souvenir from Constantinople, which may have been presented to Samuel Pepys by a Turkish envoy. (Closed 21.5 x 11.5cm.)*

17 *Trade card of a pocket book seller, 1730s.* ▷ *Showing a shagreen pocket book with the scalloped flap and ornate metal clasp popular in the second quarter of the century. Sold with an accompanying pencil. Note that in the French version, 'pocket book' is translated as* porte lettres *('letter case'). Below the bottles and snuffboxes are two chatelaines with chains and fitments.*

H. Pugh
In Raquett-Court Fleet-Street,
London.

Makes and Sells all sorts of Curiosities, in
Gold, Silver, Amber and Tortoise-shell.
Viz. Instrument Cases, Tooth-pick Cases,
Snuff Boxes, Essence Bottles, all sorts
of Canes, Shagreen Pocket Books &c.

H. Pugh dans Raquette Court dans
la rue de Fleet-Street a *Londres.*
Fait, et Vend, toutes sortes de Curiositez,
en Or, Argent, Ambre, et Ecaille de Tortue,
c'est a dire Etüys d'Instruments, Etüys
de Curedents, Tabatieres, Bouteilles a Essence,
toutes Sortes de Cannes, Porte
Lettres de Chagrin &c.ᵃ

ready-printed versions of such essential information, and 1769 saw the publication of the *Ladies' Complete Pocket Book*, soon followed by a *New and Fashionable Pocket Book* and many others. In the form of tiny almanacs set into leather pocket book cases, they contained printed poems, essays, recipes, menus, songs, dances and current hackney coach fares, and some included an engraved plate showing the latest styles in hats and headdresses. Thus from the basic contents of the lady's pocket book developed the modern woman's magazine.

From early on the pocket book was also used as a container, and many were supplied with a separate compartment, set between the note book and the case. Alternatively, fragile items could be tucked between the pages of the book itself. An early eighteenth-century pocket book in the Victoria and Albert Museum, once thought to have belonged to the miniaturist, Samuel Cooper, had miniatures inserted between its pages, and one page is still inscribed 'Sr Peter Lely's son', the title to a portrait sketch long since torn out.[54] Of equal value to their owners, however, were the fabric samples stored away by the lady described in the *Gentleman's Magazine*, or the pressed violet, a gift from her sister, which Mrs Delany kept tucked in her pocket book.[55]

They were also an obvious hiding place for paper money. Sophia Western kept a bank bill worth £100 in hers, while in 1763, the *Gentleman's Magazine* reported the existence of 'a gang who lately infested the City of London . . . and picked gentlemen's pocket books, to a surprising amount'.

Many pocket books were made in leathers like shagreen or coloured morocco, with note books of fine paper, vellum, or ivory leaf, and perhaps the addition of a silver-topped pencil. The 'Samuel Cooper' pocket book is of red morocco, elaborately tooled in a formal design of interlacing ribbons, but later examples are usually plain. Trade cards of the 1720s and 1730s show pocket books with shallow scalloped flaps, and ornate silver fastenings in the form of a spring catch. This was the type that Elizabeth Purefoy sent for repair in 1741, asking to have 'Ye spring of the bolt mended that shoots thro' the clasp'[56] and many were designed with three or four

holes in the clasp to allow for the expansion of the contents. By the late eighteenth century, a tab which slotted through a leather bar was a common alternative to catches of silver or cut steel.

In 1696 'Perfum'd Pocket Books' were advertised by Barnard's Old Perfume Shop in the Hay-Market, but they were usually bought from cutlers, stationers or toymen. The fashion for tight breeches and cut-away coats for men, introduced from the 1770s, boosted the sales of slim, fitted pocket books, so that by the 1790s, many jewellers and stationers were concentrating on the making of such cases, and styling themselves first and foremost as pocket book makers. Their products became increasingly sophisticated, and could be fitted with a range of equipment including knives, tweezers, earpicks, toothpicks, compasses and screwdrivers.

Other eighteenth-century pocket books and cases were made of silk. Those of the first half of the cen-

19 Work bag, home-made, 1699. Linen and cotton twill embroidered in multicoloured worsteds with a 'Tree of Life' and oriental birds and figures. The reverse is worked in a similar pattern and the initials 'E.M.' (45.5 x 65cm.)

◁ 18 Letter case or pocket book, 1780-1800. Paper covered with white silk crêpe, embroidered with laid cord, pink silk ribbons and tamboured spangles. The central medallion of white satin features a drawing of a classical urn. Probably home-made. (Closed 18 x 11.5cm.)

tury were in the simple envelope or flapped wallet form, worked in coloured silks, metal threads, or even straw, but towards the end of the century, a new style appeared. This was shaped like a modern wallet, with two compartments on each side opening towards the centre, the division between the two extending and folding back as a scalloped flap over the top compartment. Both these and the more traditional styles can be found embroidered with the tiny flower sprigs and medallions in tambour work, chenille thread, and spangles, so popular in the late eighteenth century.

Some of these cases were fitted out just like the leather ones, and in 1779 Queen Charlotte presented Mrs Delany with a pocket case:

> The outside white satin, work'd with gold, and ornamented with gold spangles; the inside . . . is lined with pink satin, and contains a knife, sizzars, pencle, rule, compas, bodkin, and more than I can say; but it is all gold and mother of pearl. At one end there was a little letter case that contained a letter directed to Mrs. Delany, written in the Queen's own hand.[57]

This elaborate example was the work of a professional, but many others were home-made, and in the 1780s, the *Lady's Magazine* issued several patterns for embroidered pocket books.

Morocco pocket books containing printed almanacs remained popular well into the nineteenth century, and writers in the 1820s delighted in studying the social gradations of pocket books and their owners. According to William Hone, in 1828, the fashionable young lady would carry an elegant pocket book of gilt red morocco containing poetic quotations and romantic letters. The servant maid's 'old greasy red morocco' pocket book would be crammed with popular songs, a love letter, and a lucky penny with a hole in it; while the old bachelor's pocket book of worn russia-leather, would be full of newspaper cuttings, a watch paper made for him by his little grand-niece, and a sprig of jasmine once worn on the evening dress of his current idol.[58]

Punch magazine was still issuing 'Mr. Punch's Pocket Book' in a morocco case, complete with separate compartment and pencil, in the late 1870s.

FROM WORK BAGS TO RETICULES

When fine needlework was an accomplishment expected of every well-bred woman, the work box or work bag was an important accessory. Of the work bags which survive from the late seventeenth century, many were embroidered with the date and their owner's initials, and were obviously worked at home. These flat drawstring bags, in linen and cotton twill,

are decorated with the same coloured worsteds, in the same sinuous 'Tree of Life' patterns, found on many contemporary crewel-work hangings. These bags measure at least 50cm square (one in the Victoria and Albert Museum measures one metre wide when spread out) and they probably served to store the large hanks of blue, green and carmine worsteds used in such embroideries.

During the next few years, however, fashionable needlewomen extended their repertoire to include the art of knotting, which became increasingly popular throughout the eighteenth century. By this technique linen thread was wound off a small, ornamental shuttle in a series of knots or *picots*, to produce a decorative braid which could later be couched on to a fabric in a range of linear patterns. Plying this shuttle was an easy and graceful occupation which required the minimum of skill or equipment, and showed off elegant hands to good advantage. When carried in a dainty bag, the shuttle and thread could be taken anywhere, and the work continued even at the tea table. Many a formal eighteenth-century portrait shows the sitter with an exquisite tortoiseshell or ivory shuttle delicately posed in one hand, and a little knotting bag looped over the other wrist.

Naturally, these knotting bags were smaller than the earlier work bags (surviving examples are rarely more than 25cm deep), and as fashionable accessories, to be carried on the person, they were usually made of silk. Rich brocaded bags were probably made from dress remnants, while others were specially embroidered. In 1783, when the King presented Mrs Delany with a gold knotting shuttle, she used it to knot a white silk fringe for the bag which was to contain it, and clearly many women would enjoy embroidering and trimming these bags, which were a charming advertisement to their skills.

The choice of decoration was closely related to styles found on dresses and on other accessories. Those of the second quarter of the century made considerable use of metal threads and heavy floral designs which, from the middle of the century, became lighter and more naturalistic. From the 1770s, the most popular type of knotting bag was of white satin embroidered with tiny flower sprigs,

---

20 Portrait of the Duchess of Montrose, by Soldi, c.1740. She holds a fashionable knotting shuttle and a silk knotting bag. This is either brocaded or embroidered with flowers, and has a circular base of metal mesh or braid.

sparse trailing leaves, and ribbon bows of chenille thread, applied net and spangles, or the chain stitch effects of tambour work. All were finished with silk drawstring ribbons and bows.

Most of these bags were rectangular and flat, but some were shaped to a round stiffened base. In one type this was a decorative feature, and the base was covered with a basket-work pattern of metal thread embroidery, or even solid metal. A bag of Chinese painted silk in the Museum of London has a base of interlaced silver wires, while one of woven striped silk in the Metropolitan Museum has a solid silver base with repoussé decorations of flowers, birds, and scrolls. This has the mark of a German silversmith working around the middle of the century.

Certainly, many bags were professionally made, and were sold by milliners, cutlers, or toymen like Bellamy's at the sign of the Green Parrot near Chancery Lane, which, in the 1760s, sold work bags, together with housewifes and needlebooks.[59] As with purses and pocket books, however, French examples were particularly admired, and were made all the more desirable by trade embargoes on the import of French silks. When Horace Walpole was in Paris in 1765, he bought three knotting bags, and arranged for them to be smuggled into England, at the special request of Lady Hervey.

Understandably, the ubiquitous knotting bag soon proved itself a handy container for all kinds of items and accessories, so that in 1769, Lady Mary Coke noted of one woman 'She had a knotting-bag, embroidered, hanging to her arm — "tho indeed", said she "I never knott, but the bag is convenient for one's gloves and Fan" '.[60] The knotting bag was already beginning to fulfil the role of the modern handbag, despite the wearing of tie pockets.

Towards the end of the century, the revolt against the *ancien régime* was expressed in politics, art, and fashion, and by the 1790s, luxurious gowns of stiff, rich silks had been rejected in favour of softer printed cottons, and white cotton muslins, supposedly based on the flowing draperies worn in ancient Greece and Rome. When, after 1795, the waistline rose and the silhouette narrowed, these clinging fabrics revealed the natural line of the body in a way unseen for several hundred years. In 1798, Lady Louisa Stuart wrote of 'transparent dresses that leave you certain there is no chemise beneath!'[61] and although the majority of women would have been rather more conservative about their underwear, there was certainly no room beneath such dresses for bulky tie pockets. Instead, these were discarded, and the contents transferred to the knotting bag. By 1799, *The Times* was able to point to 'The total abjuration of the female pocket . . . . Every fashionable fair carries her purse in her work-bag', and to comment on 'the new custom of carrying a bag with her smelling-bottle, purse, etc.'

Knotting bags were adapted for their new role by the addition of longer carrying strings, and a new name — 'indispensables'. (Clearly women developed that notorious dependence on their handbags from very early on.)

It was on 1 November 1799 that a fashion plate in the English magazine, the *Gallery of Fashion*, first showed women in morning dress carrying these 'indispensables'. Made of cambric or silk, according to the dress, they were trimmed with gold lace and long gold cord drawstrings and tassels. Their novelty is proved by a footnote for the benefit of the uninitiated — 'Indispensables are bags, which the ladies use instead of pockets'.

In France, these bags had been in use for some time, and there they were called 'ridicules', and later 'reticules'. The origins of these names are unknown, but a link may have been seen with netted bags used by the women of ancient Rome, and the name adapted from the Latin *reticulum* meaning 'net'. Alternatively, the word 'ridicule' may have been a term of gentle mockery, like 'indispensable'. Certainly the French treated these bags with humour, for in 1799 it was fashionable to embroider them with a rebus.

The French term *reticule* would eventually dominate, but at the very beginning of the nineteenth century, this new accessory was known in England both as a 'ridicule', and as an 'indispensable'.

21 *Caricature showing the flimsy dresses of 1800. After 1795, the new fashion for high-waisted gowns in flimsy muslin made bulky pockets impossible, and a drawstring bag or 'ridicule' became a necessity.*

2

1800-1900

INVENTIVE RETICULES

Throughout the first quarter of the nineteenth century, fashionable gowns remained narrow and pocketless, so that a bag was indeed 'indispensable'. It was certainly put to a variety of uses, and at the trial of Lord Melville in 1806, one commentator noted 'rows of pretty peeresses, who sat eating sandwiches from silk indispensables'.[1]

More typical, however, was the contents of a young lady's reticule as described by the *Lady's Magazine* in 1820. Apart from the inevitable letters and writing tablet, this contained some of the first portable cosmetics, in the form of paper packets of rouge and other powders. (As these were carried loose, naturally the inevitable happened, and a treasured miniature of a handsome youth was found to be thickly coated with some of the rouge!) The writing tablet contained a love-letter on embossed paper 'bordered with hearts and darts', and there was also 'a receipt for restoring to the eyes their original lustre', 'an original treatise of the illustrious art of shoe-making', and 'an outline of a new tucker and head-dress'.

Even with the addition of a purse, reticules did not have to be substantial to carry such items, and the lightest of frames and fabrics were sufficient. Although some were made to match the colour of the jacket or pelisse, many were seen as decorative objects in their own right, rather than as mere complements to an outfit. On the contrary, while waistlines remained high, the smooth, plain upper half of the skirt was itself an ideal foil for an elaborate reticule held against it, and the years between 1800 and 1830 produced some of the most inventive designs in the history of bags.

Flat silk bags continued in use throughout the period, but in a variety of shapes. Some were rounded or pointed at the base; some, from the period of the Napoleonic Wars, in the hexagonal shape of the military sabretache; others even octagonal, but all with tassells hanging from the lower points.

Silks were plain or embroidered, and velvet seems to have been particularly popular during the second decade. Colours matched fashionable outfits. According to Ackermann's *Repository*, in 1811, the wearer of a white promenade dress and green silk spencer (a short-waisted jacket) might well sport a green silk parasol and reticule, while in 1826, a green silk dinner dress was worn with a red velvet reticule, which matched the trimmings on the hem. Other examples might be chosen to match shoes, gloves, mantle or bonnet ribbons, so there was plenty of choice.

Framed reticules seem to have become more popular in the second decade of the century, featuring clasps of silver, riveted steel, gilt metal or pinchbeck. These were fastened with a hooked catch, and released by a press button. They might be rectangular or curved, and many were finished at the sides with moulded designs in the form of sphinxes or classical lion masks, like the 'gold lion snap' described by Ackermann in 1812.

Some early reticules were made of netted silk, in true 'antique' style, but in many cases the simple drawstring tube was stretched over one or more cane hoops, so that when suspended from the drawstrings, and weighted at the bottom by the contents, or by a decorative tassel, the whole formed a double cone shape. A beautiful example in the Costume Museum at Bath is worked in horizontal stripes of purple-brown and rich peacock blue. The hoop is bound with blue silk, the drawstrings are of wide silk ribbons in both blue and purple, and the base, sides, and ribbons are trimmed with silk bows in the same colours. These netted bags, which can be as little as 10cm in diameter, probably date from the first decade of the century, although the *Ladies' Monthly Museum* of 1815 showed one of this shape in yellow and mauve silk, while, in 1826, Ackermann featured

---

22 Fashion plate from Ackermann's Repository, *1824. The model carries a tan reticule, probably made of moulded leather, in the shape of a scallop shell, with a silver chain and mount.*

34

23 *Detail from an engraving of Turnbull's Exchange, Cheltenham. Included among the umbrellas, parasols and workboxes for sale are a number of reticules hung along the back of the counter. Among them is a shell-shaped reticule like that shown in Ackermann's fashion plate of 1824.*

one made of shaded silk ribbons, to match a silk morning dress.

Knitted silk, incorporating coloured glass and steel beads was used for more sophisticated versions of the Classical bag. Simple tubular shapes patterned in horizontal stripes, sometimes with a Greek key design, and finished at the base with a single silk or

24 Framed purse, French, 1800-1820. Pale blue silk and silver thread worked in spider's web pattern and finished with a tassel of cut steel beads. The silver frame is decorated with flower urns and sphinxes' heads, motifs which became fashionable after Napoleon's expedition to Egypt in 1798. (8 x 9cm.)

bead tassel, were ·like that used by the Roman style matron in Thomas Hope's *Designs of Modern Costume*, published in 1812.[2] More romantic styles were produced in France and Germany, where a knitted bag with a stiffened, cup-shaped base was beaded with floral patterns at the top, and lattice work at the bottom, to look like a basket of brightly coloured flowers.

Germany, still an important centre for the manufacture of bags and purses, developed a large home industry in beaded bags, using glass beads from Bohemia. These bags were made of a solid bead fabric, but unlike the French sablé technique they were buttonholed or bead knitted one by one, using slightly larger beads, in an even wider range of jewel-bright colours. Working to hand-coloured patterns produced by specialist firms, men were employed to string the beads, and women to make them up, and considerable skill was required in arranging them to form the detailed, three-dimensional designs.

Bags from the early years of the century were rectangular, alternating geometric patterns and heavy cabbage-like blooms, with perhaps a row of leaf motifs at the base, shaded to look like the mouldings on a stone urn. Other popular designs included oriental figures or baskets of flowers. By 1818 at least, circular bags were also being made, worked in triangular sections which radiated from the centre in a series of repeated patterns like a kaleidoscope. Many examples of the 1820s and 1830s have highly ornate frames and chains of French pinchbeck or cut steel, and the style proved so popular that these bags were still being made well into the 1850s.

From the very first the technique spread to other countries, and Brooklyn Museum has a sampler of typical bag designs which was worked in France. Many bags were made by skilled amateurs, and Alice Morse Earle tells of a New England lady who sought to win the heart of the local parson by giving his sister one of her precious bag patterns. Unfortunately, it fell into the hands of a rival, who made a few minor alterations. After hours of work, the parson's sister produced only a meaningless jumble of colours, and the parson's affections were lost to another![3]

Circular bags seem to have been a feature of the 1820s. In 1826 Ackermann featured a 'circular reticule of ponceau [poppy red] velvet, edged with gold, and trimmed with British lace; the strings of ponceau and white satin', and of about this date are a whole range of circular drawstring bags, made by pleating a wide strip of silk to two central stiffened medallions. A very sophisticated example at The Gallery of English Costume is made of white silk with a central cameo-like motif of a white Classical figure on a red wax seal. The seal is framed by a ring of pheasant feathers which probably matched a fashionable feather muff or tippet.

This style was very easy to make, and obviously popular with the amateur needlewoman. In many cases the medallions were also home-made, featuring designs pricked or embossed on card, both popular handicrafts of the day. The Costume Museum at Bath has one such home-made bag of bright scarlet silk, roughly sewn to circular cards which are hand-painted in black, yellow and gold with a picture of a closed book, one medallion showing the front, and the other the back. The maker must have had a sense of humour, for the spine of the book bears the title *The Points of Industry Vol. I.* Never could this bright, jolly bag have contained anything so serious!

Metalwork also plays an important part in bags of this period, and some of the most remarkable are made of iron wire, drawn out almost as fine as hair. On a base of fine iron mesh these wires were wound into tight coils and arranged in wheel or flower patterns, the spaces filled with flower-shaped steel paillettes. This type of filigree iron work was first made

◁ 25 Drawstring reticule, German, c.1820. Wool, knitted with multicoloured glass beads, the base stiffened to form a basket shape. Germany developed an important industry in beaded bags during the 19th century. (Height 21.5cm.)

26 Drawstring reticule, 1820-30. Bias-cut strip of white silk taffeta gathered front and back to a medallion of stiffened card. The centre is an imitation cameo of red and white wax, surrounded by pheasant feathers. The top opening is trimmed with silk fringe and fastened with white silk ribbon drawstrings and bows. (Diameter 26cm.)

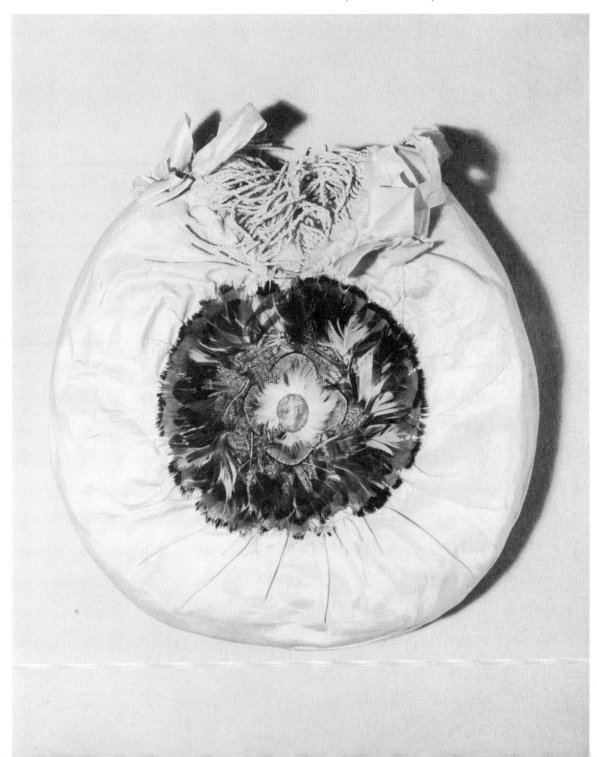

27 *Reticule, probably French, 1810-25. Steel mesh trimmed with cut steel paillettes and steel bead fringe. Top fastening by means of a loop which fits over a steel key. Some examples have an attached lining with a drawstring top. (Approx. 12cm wide.)*

in Silesia during the eighteenth century, but the War of the Austrian Succession saw the foundries moved to Berlin. After the city was captured by the French in 1806, the Prussian government called in all precious jewellery giving iron work in return, so that this material became a symbol of patriotism. During their occupation of Berlin, however, the French copied

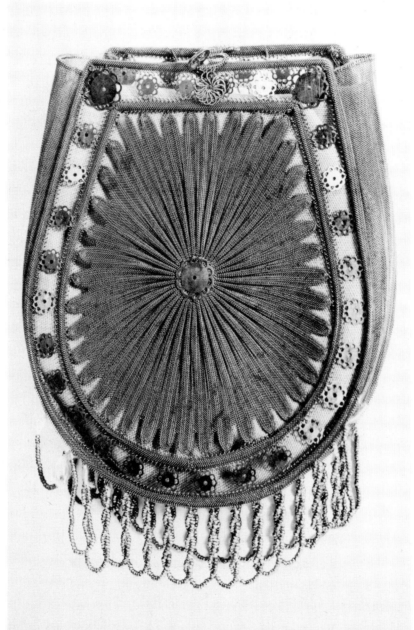

many of the designs, while other countries also experimented with the technique, so that, although generally known as 'Berlin ironwork', it is difficult to specify the origin of any one piece.

Cut steel also figures widely on bags of this period, in the form of spangles and paillettes as well as clasps and frames. In 1819 the *Journal des Dames et des Modes* described a fashion for bags of white velvet trimmed with cut steel spangles, while a circular bag of the 1820s consists of a wheel of steel hoops with panels of watered silk stretched between them. The two upper hoops can be brought together and fastened with a steel key turned in a slot, while to open the bag, they are folded back, and the fabric telescoped. Carrying strings are attached to the second layer of hoops, and the centre of each side is covered by a large cut steel button. An example in the Deutsche Ledermuseum at Offenbach has this button cut in the

shape of a flower, while each silk panel is embroidered with steel paillettes in the form of trailing stems and flowers. The whole bag is only 18cm in diameter.

Around 1815 English fashion plates show the introduction of leather reticules, which would not be out of place today. Some were simple rectangular or curved flap bags, with metal catches and plates, but in 1820 the *Journal des Dames et des Modes* described morocco leather bags made in the shape of a lyre. The Deutsche Ledermuseum has one of this shape in light brown diced calf ('Russia leather'), embossed with the ubiquitous basket of flowers

---

28 Reticule, probably French, 1815-30. Beige watered silk with steel hoops and cut steel button. Top fastening by means of a steel key which turns in a slot. (Approx. 18cm diameter.)

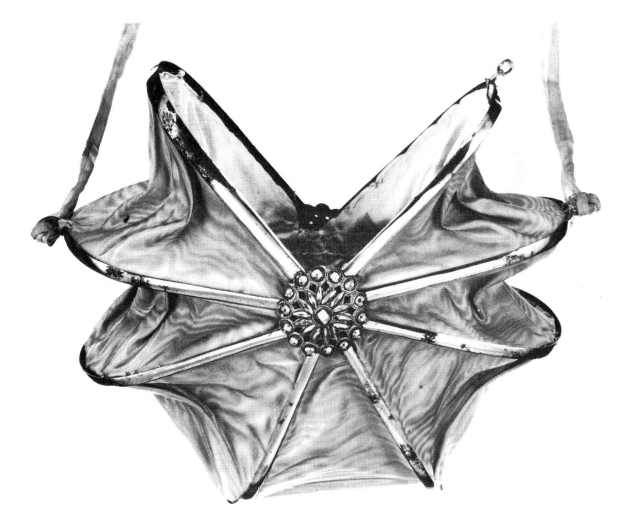

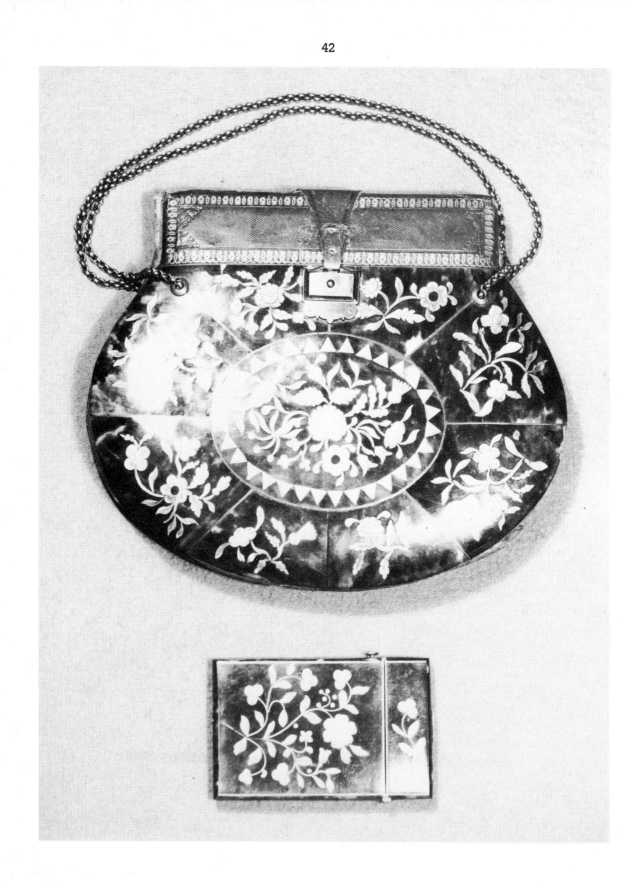

◁ 29 *Reticule, German, 1820-40. Tan diced calf, tooled in gilt, with applied tortoiseshell panels inlaid with mother-of-pearl. Steel chain and sliding catch. Two identical sections joined back to back with a leather gusset. (16.5 x 22cm.) Matching case for visiting cards.*

30 *Reticule, probably home-made, 1830-50. Black silk satin embroidered with crêpe, gauze and silk ribbon, in reds, pinks and cream. Black silk carrying ribbon with bows. Could have been carried or worn at the belt. (16.5 x 18cm.)*

highlighted with cut steel spangles. The narrow flap fastens with a palm-shaped cut steel clasp, and the handles are of plaited leather. Although probably of German manufacture, such bags were obviously available in England, for in 1823 *La Belle Assemblée* described a bag of 'fine leather, ornamented with eight plates of polished steel; the figures represented on this are the twelve signs of the zodiac'.

Equally popular in England were bags of similar diced calf, tooled in gilt, and inlaid with tortoishell panels which are themselves inlaid with mother-of-pearl. They usually consist of two identical flapped sections, joined back to back by a common gusset, which leaves a central compartment between them. The flaps are fastened with steel clasps and the compartments lined with brightly coloured silk. A

popular variety dating from the 1820s and 1830s was circular in shape with wedge-shaped panels inlaid with mother-of-pearl roses. They were sometimes made with matching cases for visiting cards.

MORE POCKETS AND RETICULES

From about 1815 the fashion pendulum had begun to swing away from clinging white muslins towards a fuller, more angular silhouette and stiffer fabrics. From 1825, waistlines dropped, skirts were filled out by increasing numbers of petticoats, and there was a revival of tie pockets.

Although similar in design to earlier examples, these pockets were regarded, like underwear, as some-thing to be kept neat, white and laundered. A few were decorated, or made in the same red flannel or brown jean as the sturdiest petticoats, but most were plain white twilled cotton. Tapes were still the usual fastening, although a few pockets were buttoned to the stays, and some had the new feature of a separate inner pocket for the watch.

As skirts grew wider, dressmakers began to stiffen them with a glazed cotton lining, and from this developed the idea of an attached glazed cotton pock-et. This soon superseded the tie pocket, and was in widespread use by the late 1840s, accompanied, in the following decade, by a small watch pocket in the front waistband of the skirt.

With the increasing use of pockets after 1830, the reticule ceased to be an object of necessity, or of high fashion. Many women continued to make them, however, both for personal use, as gifts, and as novel-ties for the growing number of charity bazaars organized by society ladies.

In the 1830s and 1840s such bags were made of silk or velvet in simple, flat, drawstring shapes, usu-ally square or flared, with a round or pointed base. In 1832, according to the *Lady's Magazine*, 'the most fashionable form is triangular', and a bag at The Gal-lery of English Costume, carried by a Manchester bride of that year, is of this shape, with the base itself extended in three sharp triangles, and the top frilled with a row of smaller 'vandyck' points. Made of white watered silk, stiffened with piped seams, it matched the white silk dress and shoulder cape.

---

31 Reticule, home-made, 1830-50. Cream velvet, hand-painted in green, brown and red. Piped with silk cord. Silk cord carrying strings and wooden tassels covered with silk. Unmade-up piece of velvet showing the same design. Painting on velvet was a popular pastime. (Reticule 16.5 x 18cm.)

Many such bags were made to match the dress or bonnet, and were hung from the belt rather than carried. Naturally they reflected dress styles very closely, and popular fabrics like challis (a silk and wool mixture), or dark silk satin, and trimmings like piping, and silk 'blonde' lace, were common to both.

The chief interest of these bags was their decora-tion, and from such sources as *The Handbook of Use-ful and Ornamental Amusements*, published in 1845, Victorian women learned the popular techniques of their day. Thus in the thirties and early forties em-broidered flowers were worked in silk in a simple cross stitch on bare linen canvas, or in applied ribbon-work, using a crewel needle to sew delicately shaded 'china' silk ribbons, only 1.5mm wide. These were used for small flowers, while chenille thread and 'penny ribbon' were used for the leaves; puffed and padded silk crêpe for larger flowers; and silk knots or beads for the centres. No detailed pattern was re-quired, and with relatively little skill one could pro-duce dramatic results, especially on a dark satin ground.

A popular technique of the forties and fifties was to paint flower designs on velvet. The fabric was prepared with diluted gum dragon, the design pen-cilled on, and the paints applied with a stiff brush, adding a touch of Indian ink for fine lines and shad-ows. The painter could make her own colours by boiling solutions of saffron, logwood chips, alum etc., but for the less dedicated, ready-made liquid colours could be bought at most drawing material ware-houses.

Beads were another easy means of obtaining sophisticated decorations. In the 1830s metal beads were worked into bags made of netting or crochet (the latter rapidly replacing netting in popularity). Colour schemes were startlingly bright. *The Lady's Magazine* of 1832 recommended gold beads with poppy red silk, and steel beads with violet. The jewel-bright, bead knitted bags were still popular of course, with their heavy flowers, or more sophisticated land-scapes, and in the 1840s sumptuous effects were achieved with metal beads embroidered on to richly coloured velvets.

The heavier fabrics were often mounted on to ornate frames of silver gilt or pinchbeck, worked with delicate flower and scroll patterns, and hung from a decorative chain, but most bags had a simple flap or drawstring fastening. They were carried by silk ribbons, or twisted silk cords, and finished with large silk tassels, the silk wound or netted over wooden acorns.

32 Framed velvet reticule, c.1850. Dark green velvet embroidered with light green silks and gilt beads, and fringed with gilt beads. Gilt metal chain and filigree frame, with a press-button catch. Women's magazines issued embroidery patterns for such bags, which were then sewn to a ready-made frame. (17 x 12cm.)

33 Beaded reticule, c.1859. Brown velvet with a stiffened interlining, embroidered with glass beads in shades of white, yellow, pink and turquoise. Edges bound with red silk, and lining of blue glazed cotton. Mauve silk carrying ribbon. Almost identical to a pattern for a North American Indian bag, featured in the Lady's Newspaper of 1859. (18 x 17cm.)

During the 1850s skirts grew increasingly wide, and by 1856 a new means of supporting them had been introduced. This was the crinoline, a huge dome-shaped petticoat made of cane or steel hoops, which enabled skirts to expand to enormous proportions, and gave the mid-Victorian woman her characteristic triangular silhouette. When distended by this petticoat, however, the line of the skirt was too smooth to allow room for a bulky pocket in the dress itself, and this promoted the greater use of the bag.

With the development of the chatelaine bag and the handbag, however (see pages 49-56) the reticule was reduced to a mere 'bag purse' or 'handkerchief reticule', and became extremely small. Many surviving examples were probably never used at all, for in 1859 the *Englishwoman's Domestic Magazine* welcomed the bag as yet another ornamental novelty suitable 'either for a contribution to a fancy fair, or for presentation to a friend' and the craze for charity bazaars in the second half of the century made the

34 *Reticules, probably home-made, 1845-70. Left, canvas embroidered with pink, cream and red wools in flamestitch embroidery. Black silk carrying cord. Tassels of pink silk and chenille, 1860-70. (16cm wide.) Right, tartan silk, in blue, black, yellow and green, embroidered with gilt thread. Silk carrying cord and tassels. Very similar to an example shown in the* Lady's Newspaper *of 1847. (14cm wide.)*

1 Drawstring purse or sweet bag, early 17th century. Canvas worked with silver thread in gobelin stitch, with a coiling stem pattern of flowers and strawberries in silk in tent stitch. Plaited drawstrings with silk-covered wooden tassels, silk and silver thread knots and tassels. (12 x 12cm.)

2 Framed purse, French, 1725-50. Linen embroidered with silk and metal threads in laid and couched work and French knots, with a picture of Diana the huntress, dressed in contemporary fashions. Square pinchbeck frame with a hooked catch. (11.5 x 9.3cm.)

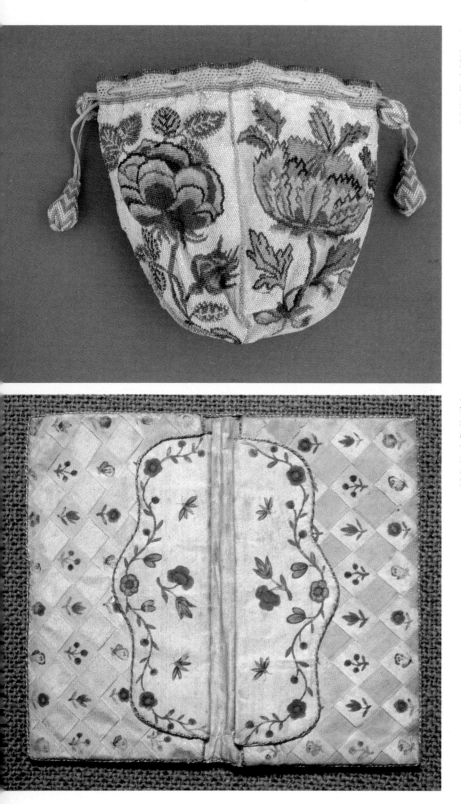

3 Drawstring beadwork purse, French, 18th century. Four wedge-shaped panels of sablé beadwork, depicting large stylized flowers in the style of the early 18th century, but otherwise identical in construction to beadwork purses of the latter part of the century. Plaited silk drawstrings and beaded wooden tassels. (Height 13cm.)

4 Inside of silk letter case or pocket book, 1780-1800. Probably home-made, from silk ribbons, interwoven and hand-painted. A double-sided, wallet-type case, with two compart-ments each side. These are divided by a silk panel which folds back as a scal-loped flap over the top compartment. (Closed, 15 x 9cm.)

production of bags, purses and other novelties almost a full-time occupation for many women.

As a result, decorative techniques were chosen for their speed of working and dramatic effects rather than their delicate craftsmanship. On flat hexagonal or horseshoe-shaped bags, glass beads were embroidered in designs of ferny leaves or fuschia-like flowers, often in a 'grisaille' palette of white, grey and black, which stood out well against a richly coloured satin or velvet. American Indian beadwork, with its brightly coloured beads worked in dramatic blocks of colour, was also popular, and in April 1859, the *Lady's Newspaper* featured a pattern of one of these 'productions of the Work-Table of the Wilderness'.

Berlin woolwork was another alternative, used in small geometric repeat patterns on tiny rectangular or pointed bags, trimmed with silk cord drawstrings and tassels. Perhaps the most characteristic style of the late fifties and sixties, however, was the use of applied gold braid in scrolling 'Turkish' designs popularized by the Crimean War. When embroidered on to a ground of velvet or cloth in emerald green, claret, dark blue or 'Turkish red', the result was bold and exotic. By the late 1860s, however, more subtle effects were being produced, using a ground of the same white cashmere then popular for dresses and jackets. An alternative to braid was the application of iridescent green 'beetle-wing' spangles as used in Indian embroidery. There were many enquiries about this technique from the 1860s onwards, and in 1865, *Queen* magazine recommended drilling them with a Walker's number eight needle, and sewing them with green silk.

Many little drawstring bags in these materials are virtually indistinguishable from the embroidered tobacco pouches which were becoming so popular, again promoted by contact with the Russians and Turks at the Crimea. The tobacco (used for home-rolled cigarettes) required a stouter fabric, however, and tobacco pouches were always lined with kid, or vulcanized rubber.

By the 1870s, the fabric reticule had been largely replaced by the chatelaine bag for both outdoor and indoor use, but the last two decades of the century saw it revived as a formal 'dress bag' (sometimes called a 'hand-bag'). Made of velvet, silk grosgrain, or plush, a favourite dress fabric of the 1880s, the usual form was a simple rectangle of material with a drawstring of tasselled silk cords, or wide silk ribbons, trimmed with large bows. Many were conscious revivals of 'the patterns of grandmother's day', and one version, called a 'Dorcas' bag, after the Biblical Dorcas who made clothes for the poor, was in the

style of the eighteenth-century work bag, with a stiffened base.

Earlier styles of decoration were revived, too, with great use of embroidered spangles, lace (now machine-made) and even ribbon embroidery (although the delicately shaded 'china' ribbons were no longer available). They differed from the originals, however, by being looser in design and more sparsely worked.

CHATELAINES AND CHATELAINE BAGS

When bags ceased to be widely used, in the 1840s, small accessories were often carried on a chatelaine. This was a much more complex accessory than the eighteenth-century version, however, for it was inspired by the mediaeval girdle and bunch of keys. Indeed, the word 'chatelaine' was first coined in the 1840s when the Victorian housewife, true to the romantic spirit of her age, saw herself as a mediaeval 'chatelaine', literally a 'mistress of the castle'.

Made of gold, silver, or cut steel, these Victorian chatelaines consisted of an elaborately worked hook from which hung a bunch of chains, each suspending some beautifully worked accessory. As useful novelties they were worn until the end of the century, and were particularly fashionable with the narrow skirts of the 1870s. At that time, shops like Mr Thornhill's in New Bond Street, sold a vast range of chatelaine attachments, including purses, scent bottles, opera glasses, bonbonnières, almanacs, fans, matches and stamp holders. Thornhill's 'Norwegian belt' could also be worn by men and fitted with 'manly accoutrements'.[4]

Chatelaines were expensive, however. Depending on the accessories chosen, the Norwegian belt cost between three and fifty guineas, and chatelaines in general use were used only by the well-to-do for indoor wear. A more practical alternative was the 'chatelaine bag', worn suspended from the waistband, and when the introduction of the crinoline, in the late 1850s, saw the revival of bags, this was the most popular style.

Like most fashions of this period, chatelaine bags seem to have been worn first in Paris, but by 1861, they were being featured in the *Englishwoman's Domestic Magazine*, who saw their origins as 'somewhat Scotch and somewhat oriental'. These early versions, usually worn with the informal bolero-style *zouave* jacket and skirt, were small flat bags, often shaped at the base to three tasselled points. Made of velvet, silk, or occasionally fur, to match the fabric or trimmings of the outfit, they were fastened with a pointed flap, and hung from the waist by a silk cord or a hook and chain.

They were to remain popular for the rest of the century, for although the wide crinoline skirt went out of fashion in the late 1860s, by 1876, fashion had swung to the other extreme, with a long tight-fitting 'cuirasse' bodice and narrow draped skirt, which again made it impossible to wear any type of hidden pocket. (The years 1876-8 saw a brief fashion for large patch pockets in the back breadths of the skirt, but when full they were both impractical and un-flattering.) This narrow silhouette continued into the 1880s, prompting *Queen* to comment in 1882:

Pockets in skirts are still impossible, for if they

---

35 Reticule or chatelaine bag, probably home-made, 1855-70. Canvas embroidered in wool in cross stitch (Berlin woolwork) in a design of red rosebuds on a yellow ground. Red and yellow silk cords threaded through gilt rings. Silk-covered wooden tassels. (Height 16cm.)

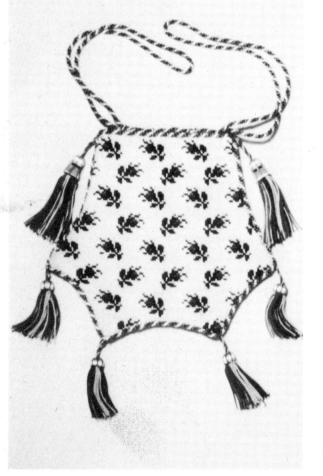

contain anything beyond the finest handkerchiefs they bulge and make themselves ungracefully apparent. The result is that chatelaine bags are adopted by those who may require to carry card-case and purse, besides the necessary handkerchief.

As skirts filled out with the bustles of the mid eighties, and the simple A-line of the nineties, attach-ed pockets were revived once more, but their disad-vantages were recognized by writers on etiquette such as Lady Viola Greville, who commented in 1892:

The average woman . . . still carries her purse in her hand, and dives into the recesses of an impos-sible receptacle, situated somewhere in the back breadths of her gown, for her pocket-handkerchief, her letters, her notebook, her card-case, or her money — the whole forming a disagreeably hard aggregation on which she patiently elects to sit.[5]

Thus bags were still retained for occasions when a larger container was required, or for formal wear, to preserve the smooth lines of a silk or muslin gown.

In the second half of the nineteenth century, bags became increasingly specialized, with more obvious differences in style between those used outdoors for travelling and visiting, and those used for indoor and formal dress. In chatelaine bags this division was already apparent by 1863, when *Queen* noted that, for travelling, chatelaine bags were 'made of leather and studded with steel', while 'for home wear they are made of gimp or embroidered velvet'.

Throughout the 1860s, indoor chatelaine bags remained small, and were often indistinguishable from other fabric bags and purses. In 1868, for example, *Queen* showed a white cashmere 'card purse', for visiting cards, embroidered with blue and red silk and applied gold cord. Its three-pointed base was trimmed with gold tassels, and it had gold draw-strings. It was recommended for hanging at the waist, as a chatelaine bag but could equally have been carried. Other dual-purpose bags were made of Berlin woolwork or, particularly in the latter half of the decade, embroidered ticking.

With the long, hip-moulding bodices of the late 1870s, many fabric bags were attached to broad sashes slung diagonally across the hips, but an alter-native was a heavy silver chain and hook attached to the belt. Black velvet pouches gathered to chased silver frames were worn in this way, and this style,

---

36 Fashion plate from the Tailor and Cutter, *1875. ▷ The model wears the narrow swathed skirts fashion-able from 1875-80, and has a flared leather chatelaine bag chained around her waist.*

The Tailor and Cutter Type of Costume.   PLATE XVI.

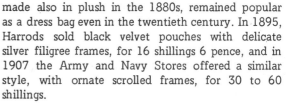

made also in plush in the 1880s, remained popular as a dress bag even in the twentieth century. In 1895, Harrods sold black velvet pouches with delicate silver filigree frames, for 16 shillings 6 pence, and in 1907 the Army and Navy Stores offered a similar style, with ornate scrolled frames, for 30 to 60 shillings.

For outdoors, leather remained popular, with sealskin a favourite in the late sixties and seventies. At this time *Queen* ran an exchange column for its readers, and in 1868, 'Tif' offered 30 shillings' worth of onyx beads to anyone who would send her 'a sealskin bag to hang at the waist, or if not sealskin, morocco'.

In the mid 1870s, exotic flared shapes were popular, reminiscent of mediaeval styles, and indeed a French leather bag of this date, at Worthing Museum, has an applied copper panel embossed with an 'antique' hunting scene. Other bags of this type which survive also have flap fronts and a distinctive scissor-shaped fastening.

The dressiest outdoor chatelaine bags were sometimes made of velvet, although on plain practical frames, while in the 1890s, a fur trimmed hat and mantle might have a matching fur chatelaine bag, complete with the animal's head and tail. For shopping and travelling, however, leather bags with inner pockets, outside 'ticket pockets' and sturdy locks and fastenings, were popular throughout the last quarter of the century. Some were supplied with their own leather belts, and this style was still being advertised as a 'tourist bag' in 1907.

FROM CARRIAGE BAGS TO HAND BAGS
In 1843 there were about 2000 miles of railway lines in Great Britain. Seven years later there were 6500, linking all the major towns in the country. Passenger transport was being revolutionized, and the age of rail travel had begun.

Although speedier than the old horse-drawn coach, long rail journeys were still relatively comfortless, however, and hours spent in carriages without heating, lighting, or refreshment facilities, prompted a demand for a handy 'carriage bag' or 'travelling wallet' for immediate necessities. The problem was

37 Flapped chatelaine bag, French, 1870-80. Brown leather with applied copper plaque showing an 'antique' hunting scene. Scissor-shaped sliding catch. Leather strap and metal hook plate to attach to the belt. (Depth 11.5cm, total length with belt mount 24.25cm.)

summed up by the *Lady's Newspaper* in 1858:

In the days of increasing locomotion, the Wallet is a necessary appendage in the hands of all ladies who travel. Whatever may be the amount of luggage, it is always inaccessible during the period of a journey, and though everything may seem to have been most carefully collected and packed up, within the deep recesses of the great black box, and well secured with lock and key, yet the trifles . . . render the Wallet highly necessary as a receptacle for all.

As early as 1826, Pierre Godillot of Paris had invented a light-framed travelling bag made of canvas, and this type of bag was revived for the English traveller of the 1850s. Naturally, being canvas, it lent itself to home embroidery in the fashionable Berlin woolwork, and vast numbers of patterns for carriage bags were published at this time, some with appropriate designs of railway engines. Once embroidered, the finished canvas was lined with tough cotton ticking and taken to the local saddler to be mounted with sturdy leather sides and handles, and a metal catch.

Because of their cheapness and durability, these woolwork, or 'carpet' bags became popular not only with the fashionable traveller, but also with those who needed nothing larger to contain all their worldly goods. As such they were widely used by emigrants to North America, and it was there, after the Civil War of 1861-5, that the word 'carpet-bagger' became a derogatory term, used to describe those immigrants from the Northern to the Southern states, whose 'property qualification' in elections consisted of nothing more than the contents of their carpet bag.

By the 1850s, the increase of travel in Britain was producing a range of more sophisticated leather luggage, including all-leather carriage bags, and in a patent of 1856, (No. 2578) these were described as 'hand-bags', presumably to distinguish them from the bulkier luggage. From the end of the decade they began to appear in formal portrait photographs, carried by middle-class women in outdoor dress, and they were widely used when travelling, visiting, or shopping, throughout the second half of the century.

The basic style, as it appears in the early photographs, was a rectangular framed bag, with rounded corners, a short stout leather handle, and an outside pocket which was covered by a deep flap with two metal catch fastenings. In the fifties and sixties, these bags often had a simple main catch, set just under the centre of the frame, but as travellers demanded greater security for all types of luggage, there was a flood of patents for new frames and fastenings. By the mid 1870s, a popular type was a silver or gunmetal frame with a heavy tubular sliding catch, released by squeezing together the ends of the tube. In the next two decades this was superseded by a neater sliding block or button. Other bags had a proper lock and key set into the top of the frame.

For travelling, large versions of this handbag remained popular well into the 1900s, and were included in fashion plates from the 1870s, where they were usually depicted on the bench of the railway waiting room. It must have been in just such a large black leather handbag that Oscar Wilde's Miss Prism in *The Importance of Being Earnest* deposited the infant Ernest Worthing (in mistake for the manuscript of her three-volume novel), leaving the bag in the cloakroom of Victoria station.[6]

Other versions of the handbag were made for more specialized uses. In 1868, H.J. Cave and Sons of Edwards Street, Portman Square, a leading stationer and luggage wholesaler, advertised leather handbags specifically designed to carry equipment or specimen boxes 'for the naturalist or amateur artist'.[7] In the 1870s, the growing popularity of the seaside produced a range of leather 'bathing dress bags', lined with waterproof cloth, while the introduction of day return railway tickets, and the growth of the great department stores, made the shopping bag a fashionable accessory. In 1897 Louis Vuitton was advertising a flat, square-framed 'hand bag' as 'the lightest and handiest shopping bag made'.

In the last quarter of the century, smaller, more elegant versions of the handbag became an alternative to the reticule or the chatelaine bag. From the late 1860s, many had been combined with fur muffs, and in 1868 Asser and Sherwin were selling 'muff-bags' mounted on an ormolu frame with a central fastening. Fitted with a short fur handle and a pocket at each end for the hands, they cost from 25 shillings to 3 guineas.[8] This style was to become still more popular with the large plush or satin muffs of the 1880s.

Small leather bags were also becoming fashionable. In 1879 Parkinson and Gotto of Oxford Street recommended morocco handbags as Christmas gifts, while other examples of that date were made in sealskin to match fashionable capes and trimmings.

These were still soft-edged bags with rounded corners, but the tailored bodice, angular bustled skirt, and sharply pointed hat of the mid 1880s popularized a hard-edged, boxy style of bag. Many were covered in red or blue plush to match the outfit, but others were made in a new range of coloured leathers.

Aniline dyes, whose development had revolutionized textile colours in the 1850s, had been adapted for leather in the late seventies, enabling leather handbags to be made in high fashion colours. A calf and morocco bag of about 1887, in the Museum of Leathercraft, is dyed in the same deep maroon found in so many dresses of the period.

With the dark tailored jackets and skirts worn outdoors in the 1890s, however, colours became more subdued, and green morocco was the popular leather of this decade. By this time, fashionable handbags were often extremely small. The Gallery of English Costume has one of dark blue leather, lined with cream kid, which was a present to Jessie Slater

◁ 38 Fashion plate from Harper's Bazaar, 1894. The model wears a French travelling outfit and carries a drawstring silk 'dress bag'. Beside her is a flapped leather 'hand bag' with a metal sliding catch, typical of the style used for railway hand luggage throughout the second half of the 19th century.

39 Framed handbag, 1887. Fawn leather covered with red plush, and embroidered in silk to commemorate Queen Victoria's Golden Jubilee. White metal frame and sliding catch, released by squeezing the two ends of the clasp. (18 x 18cm.)

from her Aunt Jane, in 1897, and measures no more than 13 by 14cm.

As bag construction became more sophisticated, however, specialist bags were produced, already fitted out for specific occasions. Thus a 'visiting bag' advertised in *Queen* in 1897 contained its own purse, visiting-card case, and scent bottle. A 'matinée bag' was also fitted with a scent bottle, opera glasses and biscuit case, while an 'opera bag' contained opera glasses and a powder puff. (The use of powder was only just becoming acceptable, but both this and the double-ended bottles for scent and smelling salts were very necessary in a crowded Victorian theatre.)

MORE PURSES AND POCKET BOOKS

In the first half of the nineteenth century most purses were home-made, and displayed the same techniques as those used for bags. Netting was popular in the early years, and Mr Bingley in *Pride and Prejudice* was impressed by the fact that all accomplished young ladies could 'paint tables, cover screens and net purses'.[9] Many of these purses were simple tubular bags, weighted by a tassel at the bottom and fastened with a drawstring, or mounted on a press-button frame of steel, silver, or pinchbeck. The most usual type, however, was a dainty, cobweb-fine version of the wallet purse, rarely more than 15 to 20cm long. Of plain or steel-beaded silk mesh, it was fitted with tassels and sliders of mother-of-pearl, ivory, silver filigree or pinchbeck, sometimes painted with enamels.

This wallet purse, known by this time as a 'long purse', or simply a purse, was the most popular type in use until the 1860s, and was made in a variety of materials. Around 1800 it could be found in printed kid; by the twenties and thirties in bead knitting, or red silk, with 'vandyck' points; and during the next two decades in embroidered silk or velvet. The majority of Victorian examples, however, are about 30cm long, and worked in crochet or knitting, in silk or cotton thread and gilt or steel beads. Although coarser than the earlier netted purses, their stitches are still fine by our standards, and were often knitted on size 18 needles. They were trimmed with matching sliders and elaborate tassels of metal beads and bugles. Some were made with one end square and fringed, so that gold coins placed in one half could be distinguished from silver at the other. They were used by both sexes, and although patterns were sometimes specified as being for a gentleman or a lady, there was no obvious difference in style.

Brightly coloured bead knitted purses, mounted on small pinchbeck frames, were made as miniature versions of the beaded reticules. Others were made in hexagonal form with a pointed flap, or as flat rectangles with silk threads passing through a flap and attached to a finger ring, so that when the purse was carried, the strings pulled it closed. From a tiny tubular 'penny purse', closed by a drawstring or slider just below the top, developed the jug-shaped purse whose slider gathered the fabric into a 'neck', and was attached to the body by a loop of cord reminiscent of a jug handle. Later in the century, many novelty 'jug purses' were knitted in jug shape, their decorative stitches imitating the effects of cut glass.

The introduction of the tiny gold sovereign in 1816 inspired the making of individual, round, 'sovereign purses', mounted on tiny curved metal frames. Usually worked in netting or crochet, although sometimes commercially made in morocco or suede, they measure no more than 3cm in diameter.

Although most purses were used for money, some were made specifically to contain visiting cards. Those of the late 1840s were often made of crochet or beaded velvet, on curved metal frames, while those of the late sixties might be of braided cloth, closed with a drawstring and worn chatelaine style.

From the mid 1850s, however, the growing popularity of leather bags was reflected in a greater use of leather purses. In 1854 *The Ladies' Book of Fancy Work* featured an embroidered leather 'porte monnaie' which could be worked at home and taken to a case-maker to be mounted on a hinged metal frame. The example shown featured a new type of fastening in the form of an exterior, square-sectioned clip, mounted on a swivel-pin, which lowered over the two halves of the frame and clipped them together. (This was soon found to be too insecure for a main fastening, but it was widely used for purse compartments, well into the twentieth century.)

By the 1860s, framed purses could be bought ready-made, and in a wide variety of materials. According to *Queen* in 1865, London shops were selling purses of morocco leather; tortoiseshell 'richly gilt in arabesque and dotted patterns'; painted 'Russia' leather; malachite; and ormolu bordered with enamel, while surviving examples from this date include ivory, lacquer, mother-of-pearl, and solid silver. The

---

40 *'The Empty Purse', painted by Collinson, 1857. The subject is a beaded 'wallet' or 'long' purse, the round end trimmed with a metal tassel, and the straight end with a fringe. The girl holds one of the metal sliders in her other hand. Such purses were made in vast numbers for church fêtes and bazaars.*

41 19th-century purses. Top, silver purse with finger ring, 1898-9. Left, shaggy bead purse of pink silk, knitted with glass and steel beads, like that featured in the Ladies' Knitting and Netting Book, 1839. Centre and below, two leather purses, one with a portrait in lacquer, 1860-70, the other decorated with flowers in enamels. Right, mother-of-pearl purse, with finger ring, 1890s. Below right, sovereign purse, embossed gilt metal, containing a spring-loaded disc to hold the coin, late 19th century. (Diameter 3cm.)

favourite shape was rectangular with rounded corners and a scrolling top. The main fastening was a press-button catch, but the inside, lined with brightly coloured silks, was often divided into a number of compartments, the centre section fastened by the swivel clip. One novel variation was a purse made of a large bivalve shell, complete with silk lining and compartments. Said to have appeared first at the Great Exhibition, many were sold as souvenirs at popular seaside resorts.

By the 1870s, fabric purses had virtually disappeared, and from then on most examples were made in plain leather, or the same materials as fashionable handbags. Plush was popular in the 1880s, morocco, lizard and crocodile in the 1890s, and fur in both decades.

Many of the soft leather or plush purses were mounted on frames with the new 'twist knob' fastening, and this style was to remain popular for women's handbag purses throughout the twentieth century. Alternatively, flapped purses were used by both sexes. In 1895, Harrods sold them with silver corners and catches, in small sizes for men and large for women, and by 1907 many had separate compartments for silver and gold coins.

From the late 1890s, when dresses were cut to fit smoothly over the hips, it was impossible to have pockets in flimsy summer gowns or elaborate evening dresses, and there was a revival of the wallet purses which could be twisted round the forefinger. These and other small fabric purses with metal mounts, were also popular for card counters. (Indeed, wallet

---

42 *Purses, 1850-1900.* Top, *French purse of striped linen and silk in green, purple and cream, with purple paper lining. Brass frame and base, marked* 'PARIS EXPOSITION UNIVERSELLE, 1867'. *(Width 9cm.)* Bottom, *bivalve shell with metal hinge and clasp, inner compartments of scarlet leather. A popular souvenir sold at the Crystal Palace and seaside resorts, 1860-90. (Width 11cm.)* Right, *steel framed purse with sliding catch, open to show green moiré silk lining and popular swivel clip fastening to inner compartments, 1850-70.*

Combined

Sovereign Purse

and

Match Box.

No. 192.

Silver 15/0

Combined Sovereign and Postage Stamp Case.

Plain Silver.......................... each 10/0

POCKET COMBINATION MONEY CASE.

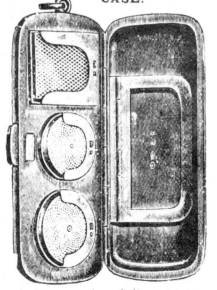

Silver, to take sovereigns, half sovereigns, postage stamps, and bank notes ... each 34/6

purses were still being used for gambling in the 1920s.) Other alternatives for dress wear were German silver or silver mesh purses, carried instead of a handbag (see pages 63-65), and these remained popular until the First World War.

Men carried sovereign purses in plain, chased or engine-turned silver, attached by a ring to their watch chain. Some were made in the style of a watch case, with a spring clip which could hold up to five coins. Others were tubular and held groups of sovereigns and half-sovereigns side by side. By 1907, leather versions included the German 'breast purse', containing a leather tablet with nine coin pockets. This was slotted into a chamois bag to be worn securely around the neck of the wary traveller. These styles continued until 1914, when the gold sovereign was finally replaced by the one pound paper bank note.

At this time, coin purses for men included the horseshoe-shaped, flapped 'Portsea' and 'tuck' purses (the latter so-called because the flap tucked into the main body like a lid), but as paper money began to replace coins, greater use was made of the pocket book. This had been carried, with or without attached almanac or note book, throughout the nineteenth century, and from the 1850s at least, the double-sided version was also known as a 'wallet', recalling the earlier double-ended bag. Pocket books and wallets really came into their own during the 1914-18 war, however, partly because of the new one pound note, but also because uniformed soldiers required slim pocket-sized cases for documents and papers. Wallets became more specialized, and by the end of the war there were cases for 'treasury notes', 'season tickets' and 'ration books'. In the 1920s, multi-pocketed wallets were seen as 'a boon to the man of affairs'[9], while in the thirties, increasing travel saw them extended to include 'motor licence' and 'passport' cases.

---

43 *Sovereign purses, 1907. Illustrated in the* Army and Navy Stores Catalogue *of that year.*

3

1900-1980

PURSE BAGS AND DOROTHY BAGS

In the years before the First World War, middle-class women extended their range of activities in many fields. They made excursions by rail, bicycle, and the new motor car, took up a variety of sports, began to demand the right to academic education, or in many cases, earned their own living as typists, governesses, or shop-girls. For the bag trade they provided a new market, and by 1907 a range of document case styles was offered as 'a novelty for the business woman, suffragette, lecturer, or any lady who has private papers, notes, cards, etc. to carry with her'.[1]

Until that year, the fashion for full curvaceous figures, padded hips, and flared skirts, allowed the wearing of pockets except in the flimsiest of summer chiffons, yet in 1902, it was noted that 'Many women seem unable to exist without a satchel of some kind'.[2] After 1907 a new 'Directoire' fashion, with a raised waistline and narrow skirt, recalled the styles of the early 1800s, and had the same effect in promoting the use of the handbag, in a variety of styles.

By then, even among the more conservative, practical tailor-made outfits were as common in the wardrobe as frothy afternoon gowns or sumptous evening dresses, and a range of bags was necessary to suit each type of costume.

For travel the large leather 'hand bag' was still available, and a more specialized version was the fitted 'motor bag'. Chatelaine 'tourist bags' were worn by both men and women, but for the woman who travelled alone, and feared for the safety of her money and jewels, there was an 'underskirt safety bag'. This was a type of tie pocket, made of suede or stout fabric, on a webbing belt, and fitted with a twist knob purse, or flapped compartments. In the same vein was the 'Keptonu' chamois leather garter, with attached pockets. The equally topical problem of safeguarding one's purse while playing tennis or skating was solved in a similar way by the 'Here it is pocket' or 'Rink-O bag', which was clipped to the waist, or buttoned to the underskirt.

For wear with smart tailored costumes, there was a wide range of smaller leather bags on silver or gun-metal frames, reflecting the view that 'a really good leather or suede handbag may not be particularly smart, but it is never in bad style, while it has the advantage of being useful'.[3] Before 1907, these leather bags were rarely more than 15cm wide, yet most were fitted with an inner purse division, or a matching purse, often attached by a chain to the bag itself. These 'purse bags' were usually rectangular, with a flap or twist knob fastening, and carried by a leather handle or metal chain. Many had especially long handles which could be looped round the wrist for safety.

They were made in a wide range of leathers from smooth chamois to scaly crocodile or lizard, and many cheaper leathers were stamped in imitation of the more expensive skins. Although imported from all over the world, almost all bag leathers at this time were dyed in Germany, whose vast chemical industry was able to produce an impressive range of colours. Even the cheapest bag at 2 shillings 11 pence might be available in red, sky blue, mauve, heliotrope, champagne, royal blue, pink, and green, and in 1904 there was a vogue for white.

Despite their size, most bags were fitted with at least a card case and writing tablet, and from 1904 some had a watch set into the front. Although few ladies would admit to the use of rouge and eyelash make-up outside the confines of the boudoir, powder was accepted, and a range of 'vanity bags' were specially fitted with a large mirror, powder puff and scent bottle.

By 1907, bags were already growing larger, with curved 'balloon' frames, or waisted frames in the 'modern' style, and the range of fittings expanded to match. The 'Ascot bag' of that year contained a framed purse, mirror, cut-glass scent bottle, bonbonniere, and a powder puff in a drawstring bag.

After 1907, Directoire fashions promoted a range of novelties. In 1908 there was a vogue for soft leather drawstring 'Dorothy bags', or 'Squaw bags' with leather fringes. Mappin and Webb, the London

44 Fitted opera bag, French, c.1910. Boxy flapped bag of beige leather, lined with silk, and fitted with twist knob purse, mirror, ivory writing tablet and gold pencil, opera glasses, folding fan, and swansdown powder puff. Long beige silk carrying cord with tassels. (Closed — 17cm high x 10.5cm wide.)

---

jewellers, popularized a morocco 'sabretache bag' on long tasselled cords, while a 'Directoire bag' of green or grey suede was a 'quaint basket-shaped reticule'[4] threaded with matching ribbon. In the same year, Liberty's imported a range of Japanese bags, the leather embossed with oriental designs, and one type was 'suspended by a number of short dulled steel chains from a metal knob handle'.[5] Surviving examples show these to be versions of the Japanese pouch and netsuke, delicately worked in ivory and silver.

With the hobble skirts of 1910, there was a fashion for bags nearly 30cm square, which looked still larger by comparison. Many had very long handles or cords and were worn by some women 'slung across the shoulders as the postman carries his satchel'.[6] As

SLAVES OF FASHION

45 Caricature from Punch, 1910, mocking the new craze for large handbags.
Ethel — 'Lend me your hanky, Mabel.'
Mabel — 'Haven't you got one in your bag?'
Ethel — 'Good Gracious, my dear girl, do you think I should put anything in this bag? It's as much as I can carry empty!'

these bags grew in size, they generally became plainer, and in one popular style the front was completely hidden by a deep flap.

For afternoon visits and dressier occasions, a tiny silver chain purse, lined with chamois leather, was often all that was carried. By 1907, the Army and Navy Stores was able to offer a wide range of these, including a soft drawstring version, as well as framed purses with a twist knob clasp. These might be carried by a chain and finger ring; pinned to the dress; or attached to a chatelaine belt by a ring on the frame. Again most were imported from Germany, then the major centre for metal bag frames and fittings, and the most elaborate had engraved clasps and a silver bead fringe. These ranged in price from 30 to 60 shillings, but gun metal was used for cheaper versions, while at the top end of the market, Mappin and Webb stocked gold mesh bags whose frames were inset with diamonds and rubies.

Other purses were made in solid metal, and carried by a metal chain. In 1908, Mappin and Webb showed a silver vanity case only 4.5 by 5.5cm, fitted with a miniature powder puff, mirror, and a clip for visiting cards, while in 1912, Hunt and Roskill, the London silversmiths, sold one in the form of a tiny metal apple.[7]

An alternative for dressier occasions was the fabric bag, either set on a metal frame with a chain handle, or in the form of the 'Dorothy bag'. This was a long rectangle of fabric with a drawstring ribbon, usually set a little below the top to form a frill. Like its predecessor, the 'Dorcas bag', it was easily constructed, light to carry, and could be made of the same fabric as the dress. It, too, had romantic associations with homely needlewomen and rustic virtues, the name Dorothy having been popularized in 1880 by A.J. Munby's play of that name, whose subject was a simple country wench. This may have given it an additional appeal to those devotees of the simple stitches and stylized forms of 'Artistic Needlework', who embroidered Dorothy bags to match 'artistic' gowns.

Richer versions were made for evening wear, however, using silk brocades or lavishly embroidered velvets, and commerically made opera bags were advertised in this style with a mirror set into the base.

After 1907, large fabric bags were ideal with slim Directoire dresses, and styles became bolder and more exotic. In 1909 a bag of white ribbed silk covered with thick Irish crochet or cheaper machine-made lace was recommended with light summer dresses of lace and chiffon, while for evening, Self-ridges of Oxford Street stocked a range of Viennese bags, beaded and sequinned on silk or gold tissue, and mounted on filigree frames of oxydized silver, set with semi-precious stones. By 1911 the fashion for oriental motifs, promoted by Poiret, and by the Russian Ballet's performance of 'Scheherezade', expressed itself in the use of tassels and scrolling designs in applied braid. On the eve of the First World War, women wore softly draped gowns and witty little hats very similar in mood to those of the early nineteenth century, and large fabric bags with exotic bead embroidery and long fringes recalled the early reticules.

SILVER CHAIN PURSES.

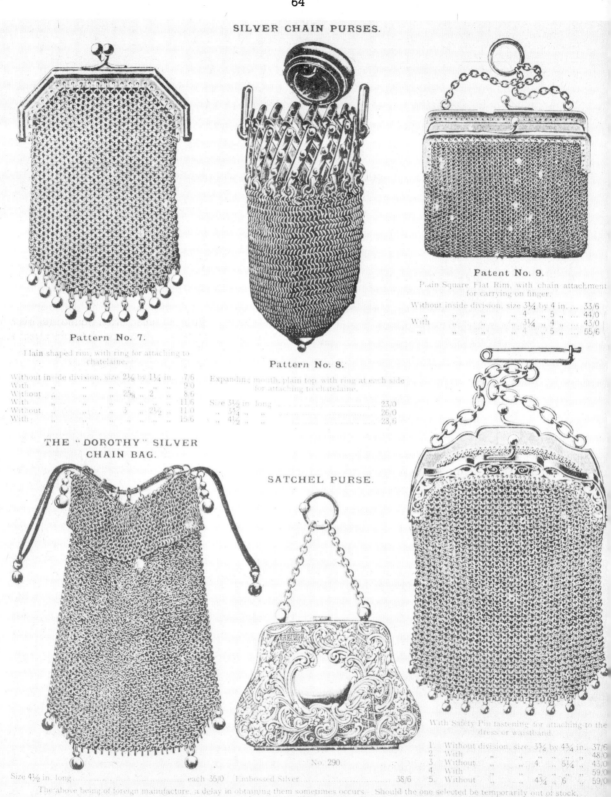

Pattern No. 7.

Plain shaped rim, with ring for attaching to chatelaine.

Without inside division, size 2⅜ by 1¾ in.						7/6
With	,,	,,	,,	,,		9/0
Without	,,	,,	,, 2⅝ ,, 2	,,		8/6
With	,,	,,	,,	,,		11/6
Without	,,	,,	,, 3 ,, 2½	,,		11/0
With	,,	,,	,,	,,		15/6

Pattern No. 8.

Expanding mouth, plain top, with ring at each side for attaching to chatelaine.

Size 3½ in. long		23/0
,, 3¾ ,,		26/0
,, 4½ ,,		28/6

Patent No. 9.

Plain Square Flat Rim, with chain attachment for carrying on finger.

Without inside division, size 3¼ by 4 in.					33/6
,,	,,	,,	,, 4 ,, 5 ,,		44/0
With	,,	,,	,, 3¼ ,, 4 ,,		43/0
,,	,,	,,	,, 4 ,, 5 ,,		55/6

THE "DOROTHY" SILVER CHAIN BAG.

Size 4½ in. long. .... each 35/0

SATCHEL PURSE.

No. 290

Embossed Silver 38/6

With Safety Pin fastening for attaching to the dress or waistband.

1.	Without division, size, 3¼ by 4¾ in.					37/6
2.	With	,,	,,	,,		48/0
3.	Without	,,	,, 4 ,, 5¼ ,,			45/0
4.	With	,,	,,	,,		59/0
5.	Without	,,	,, 4¾ ,, 6 ,,			59/0

The above being of foreign manufacture, a delay in obtaining them sometimes occurs. Should the one selected be temporarily out of stock, the nearest will be substituted.

◁ 46 *Silver chain purses and bags, 1907. Illustrated in the* Army and Navy Stores Catalogue.

47 *Dorothy bag, 1919. Black silk satin with pointed 'capes'. Embroidered with metal beads, some of which are tinted pink or green. Silk drawstring slotted through crochet-covered rings. Pink silk lining. The year 1919 saw the fashion for tasselled points on dresses, too.*

PLASTICS AND POCHETTES

By 1914, with the backing of Germany's extensive chemical and metal industries, the area around Offenbach-am-Main had become the leading producer and exporter of top-quality leather handbags, and held a virtual monopoly of the British market.

With the outbreak of the First World War, Britain found to her cost the extent of her reliance on German goods. Although government help was forthcoming in the establishment of a chemical industry, and 1916 saw the recall of hundreds of chemical workers who had joined up in the first years of the war, Britain had neither the time nor resources to achieve German standards of expertise. The British bag industry could not hope to compete.

Although the supply of handbags was seriously affected by the war, the demand was not. On the contrary, the market for luxury bags remained un-

diminished, while a new market was created among women doing war work, many of whom had left poorly paid domestic service and were earning far better wages as munition workers.

Attention was focussed on French goods and styles. In Paris fancy goods stalls proliferated, catering to the needs of soldiers returning from the front, and in search of presents for wives and girlfriends. Some retailers began to specialize in handbags. Others featured work done by wounded soldiers, which included bags made from cast-off gloves, or dress remnants, often exquisitely embroidered or beaded.

All these circumstances combined to further promote the use of fabric bags, and those of the war years closely reflected the shapes and materials of current dress styles. In 1914, when dresses were still narrow and draped, the vogue was for long oval-shaped bags in silk or velvet, with vertical stripes or pleats. Even where leather was occasionally used, it was a soft skin such as puma calf, pleated and frilled like a textile. With the fuller, often flounced skirts of 1916, silk bags were wider, topped by an attached 'cape' or 'petals' of the same fabric. Three years later, when dresses with handkerchief points were all the rage, these 'petals' were also long and pointed, and trimmed with tassels.

Although most bags were made in the Dorothy style, a substitute for metal frames was found in the use of tortoiseshell, either real or imitation, and in carved ivory from Japan.

Black was the predominant colour of war-time bags, partly relieved by bright silk or bead embroideries, but 1916 saw a Paris fashion for the green and red stripes of the *croix de guerre*. Fur was a favourite trimming for all accessories, while in 1919, fringes were popular on bags, as on dresses and parasols.

After the war, women began to exploit their new independence. Inspired by the glamour queens of the cinema they began to wear lipstick and eye make-up, and with the growing acceptance of smoking they bought their own elegant cigarette cases and holders. Despite the appearance of large patch pockets in coats and jackets from 1916, this wealth of new accessories made some sort of bag or large purse essential on all occasions (especially as dresses became shorter and skimpier in the twenties). The bag was soon treated as an integral part of a woman's total outfit, causing the *Fancy Goods Record* to comment in 1925 'Every woman wants more than one bag. She wants a useful market and shopping bag for going out with; dainty theatre and tiny vanity bags . . . . She would like one to match every costume'.

Although in Britain the leather bag industry had

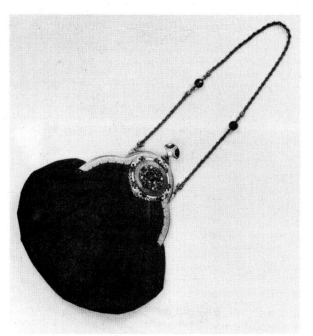

48 *Framed silk evening bag, 1920-25. Brown moiré silk, finely pleated to a gilt metal frame decorated with moulded flowers, enamels, and semi-precious stones. Chain handle set with amber beads. Lining of cream brocade, with two inside pockets.*

made rapid progress, fabric bags retained their popularity, for they allowed greater possibilities of colour and decoration to accompany a scintillating beaded evening dress, or offset a chic little suit. Plain basic colours were available, and the pouchy framed bag in 'black, navy or nigger' was carried throughout the decade, but many bags show colours and designs which reflect the whole range of popular influences on all art forms of the period.

Bags in coloured metal mesh, or in bead-work in the style of the early nineteenth century, remained popular, and French bead-embroidered reproductions were very like the originals. A flirtation with full skirts, however, in the early twenties, produced a range of bags beaded with designs of dainty eighteenth century ladies in hooped petticoats. Other designers, inspired by the Bauhaus, Cubism, and

49 *Plastic vanity bag, French, c.1925. Domed,* ▷ *hinged box, with diamanté insets. Interior fitted with mirror, powder puff and brown eye make-up. Black silk cord and tassels. (Diameter 11.5cm.)*

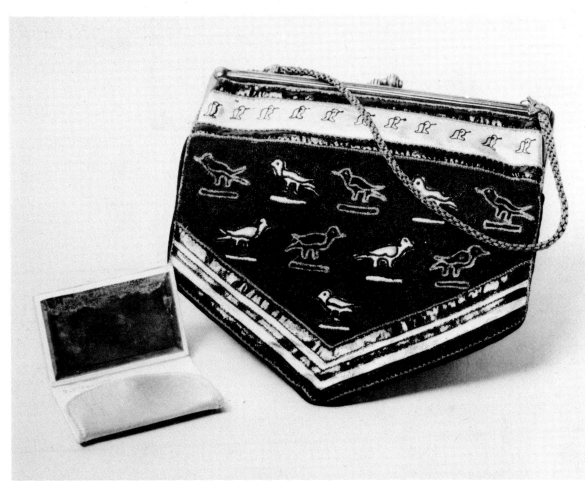

50 Framed handbag, French, c.1924. Black and gold leather and green felt, with applied Egyptian style bird motifs in gold and black. Gold braid handle. 'Futurist' lining of ruched yellow satin, with two pockets, each lined with lime green satin. (21 x 21cm.) Matching covered mirror.

Aztec art, favoured the strong colours, straight lines, and simple geometric shapes which were the main themes of the Paris Exposition des Arts Decoratifs in 1925. Their beaded bags in this Art Deco style featured stylized flowers set against jazzy stripes and checks, or purely abstract designs of scallops, pyramids and sun rays.

Even before the war, art and fashion had shown a growing interest in the exotic, and by 1920, *Vogue* could comment 'Wherever we cast our eyes, whether in dress, furniture, or house decoration we are struck by the amazing Oriental influence on European things'. This was extended to include not only styles and materials from China and Japan, but the strong colours and shapes of African art, and the decorative motifs of ancient Egypt. Scarabs, pyramids, and palms abounded, particularly after the discovery of Tutankhamun's tomb in 1923.

Already by 1914 metal twist knob clasps were appearing in the shapes of snakes, elephants, and scarabs, and the choice of exotic materials like amber, tortoiseshell and ivory, to replace diminishing supplies of metal frames was thus a natural development. Many such frames were left plain. Tortoiseshell ring handles were used for the simplest form of gathered bag, while silk pouches were given curved or ogee-shaped ivory frames, fastened by a large press-button, and often supplied with a monogrammed tab. Others developed the fashion for novelty frames by the use of Japanese carved ivories, whose designs became increasingly complex. In 1920, one journal declared that, to be fashionable, a frame must now show not

one elephant, but 'a whole troupe of elephants.'[8]

These materials were expensive. In 1920, tortoise-shell framed bags cost around £7, plain ivory from £11 to £13, and blonde tortoiseshell as much as £24. Manufacturers were quick to substitute imitations, using some of the early plastics, which could be impressed or moulded with surface designs to imitate hand-carving. British products included Lactoid, Erinoid, and Galalith, based on casein, a protein derived from milk, while Xylonite, a popular sub-stitute for ivory, was a form of cellulose acetate. Similar materials were produced in Germany, France, and Japan itself, but most of the surviving examples in English museums appear to have been made in France. These plastics were considerably cheaper than the original materials, and in 1922, Marshall and Snelgrove advertised silk bags with imitation shell and ivory frames for only 25 shillings 6 pence.

The cult of the exotic extended even to bag lin-ings. In 1916 these might be made of bright silk, with maybe 'a wreath of embroidered flowers round the frame'[9], but in the 1920s, 'Futurist bags' re-vealed linings of silk or rayon dyed in startling colours. Printed or tie-dyed fabrics were also popular, and often enclosed a matching handkerchief.

Most bags had a gathered pocket in the lining, or perhaps an attached mirror, bound in the same fabric, but an alternative was the separate vanity case, which could be carried on its own in the evening, or kept in the pocket by day. In 1922, Iris Storm, the charis-matic heroine of *The Green Hat*, kept her tube of 'lip-salve' in the pocket of her leather jacket, while her powder was contained in a 'hexagonal black onyx box, initialed in minute diamond letters', and chained to a cigarette case of white jade.[10]

Cheaper versions of this fashion again made use of plastics. Ebonite, a form of vulcanized rubber, was used for dark colours, while the cellulose acetate Trolite appeared in a range of shades and was recom-mended for wireless insulation and mah jong tiles as well as vanity cases. The Gallery of English Costume has a black case of this type. A circular domed box with a diamanté inset, its hinged lid opens to reveal a moulded interior, fitted with a tiny mirror, powder puff and brown eye make-up. Only 11.5cm in diam-eter, it is hung with two black tassels, and suspended from a long black cord. Other versions have a lipstick concealed in the tassel, and one black metal case of 1925 was fitted with an electric lamp to shine on the mirror.

Novelties were not confined to vanity bags, how-ever, for according to *Vogue* in 1920, 'Sometimes an evening bag looks for all the world like a bunch of violets, but its stems pull apart and leave just room for a bit of rouge and powder and a handkerchief like a cobweb'. In the same year, even a daytime bag might consist of a 'cobweb' of leather thongs, to which 'jewelled spiders and flies can be added'.[11]

For use with chic little dresses and tailored suits, however, most women preferred a more practical handbag, although even these could be excitingly styled (especially when expensive and French). The Victoria and Albert Museum has a range of framed leather bags of the mid-twenties, whose wide trapeze shapes are slim and elegant, but which all display some witty and inventive feature. A bag of smooth black calf, on one of the new chromium frames, reminiscent of tubular furniture, suddenly swoops upwards on one side to a point like the prow of a ship, slicing across the end of a two-tone plastic handle. Another of green morocco, bought in Bond Street, is decorated with a diagonal line of leather strips, twisted to show their pale undersides like a row of piano keys, while a third in black patent leather and green fabric, is appliquéd with tiny green and gold stylized birds, like Egyptian hieroglyphs.

Perhaps the most important development of this period, however, was the introduction of a comp-letely new variation on the handbag — the 'pochette'.

In 1916, the *Bag, Portmanteau and Umbrella Trader* noted that it had become 'the thing' to carry one's Dorothy bag 'crumpled up' in the hand, and this fashion popularized the 'big purse' in the form of a flat, rectangular bag with no handle. This style caught on quickly, and was soon christened the 'pochette', or, from the popular method of carrying it while the hands were occupied, the 'underarm' bag. Some form of attachment was necessary for security, however, and by 1920 it had acquired a vertical wrist or thumb loop on the back. Although some were gathered in to curved clasps, by the mid-twenties the most popular style was the flapped rectangular bag, whose clean uncluttered lines matched the fashionable silhouette.

Attached directly to the hand it was expressive in the same way as the fan or the cigarette. Tucked neatly under the arm it gave a military hauteur, or, balanced against the hip, an air of nonchalant chic.

51 *Fashion plate from* Le Tailleur Pratique, *1929. The girl on the right carries a flapped* pochette *or 'underarm bag', whose sleek uncluttered outlines complement her clothes. The girl on the left has a traditional style handbag, but carries it like a pooh ette.*

It also provided a canvas for a whole range of fashionable decorations. The majority of bags shown in the Art Deco exhibition were of this type, and displayed work in leather appliqué, interwoven leather strips, applied metal paillettes in geometric shapes, or embroideries of stylized flowers in bold colours. These were chosen to exhibit the best of professional craftsmanship, but many devotees of popular handicrafts produced home-made versions in felt appliqué or tooled leather work.

By the late twenties, even those pochettes with a frame and top fastening had become neater in design. A single marcasite knob or bar was turned or slid to one side to release a catch, and was often so streamlined as to be barely visible. New alternatives were the 'Gripit' handle, a flat panel of imitation tortoiseshell with a curved opening for the hand, or the 'zip' fastener, first introduced into Britain in 1919, and used on bags by the mid-twenties (although it did not appear on dresses for another decade).

CRUISE BAGS AND BEADS
In the last few years of the 1920s, dress styles became more streamlined and sophisticated, with fabrics

52 Bags, 1925-40. Left, evening handbag of black mesh, tambour-beaded with glass beads in yellow, red, black and purple. Imitation ivory frame, 1925-30. Right, daytime pochette of green rexine, with chromium frame and twist-knob fastening, 1930-35. (Width 28cm.) Bottom, flapped evening bag of shell pink rayon satin, with monogram of yellow bakelite plastic. Used on a cruise in 1938.

shaped by intricate seams in asymmetrical patterns. By the early thirties, the hemline had dropped, the waist had risen, and the fashionable figure was long and willowy, moulded by soft bias-cut draperies, in crêpe and chiffon.

The slim pochette remained the fashionable bag for most of the decade. By day it appeared in geometrically patterned 'tapestry' fabrics, or distinctive leathers such as crocodile, lizard, ostrich and tapir calf, whose only decorations were parallel lines of pleats, tucks or topstitching, echoing those on clothing. Most fastened with a flap, or with an almost invisible streamlined clasp.

For afternoon and evening, these bags were made in felt or popular dress fabrics, like ottoman silk, chiffon, grosgrain and crêpe, often in the new rayon artificial silk. A plain fabric might be dressed up by the addition of one of the glittering paste clips worn on the necks of dresses, and on hats and shoes, or alternatively, the bag itself might have a diamanté mount. By 1933, top-fastening bags had catches which were released by a hinged tab or 'lifter' in the form of a diamanté clip or a large marcasite button.

By 1935, dresses with fuller skirts and the new

---

53 Bag interiors, 1925-40. Left, 'Futurist' lining of violet shot silk, edged with ruching. Gathered pocket. Attached mirror with matching binding. Right, lining of rayon moiré. Inner purse division attached to main frame, the left side lined with white moiré. Bottom, lining of shell pink rayon satin. Two flat inner pockets and one lipstick pocket piped with silver. Matching twist knob purse and bound mirror.

puffed sleeves might be accompanied by bags trimmed with little bows or frills, but in the same year, Schiaparelli, the most theatrical dress couturier of the decade, showed a matching transparent bag and shoes in Rhodophane, a derivative of glass. From then on, accessories became increasingly inventive and escapist. In 1936, the year of the first Surrealist exhibition in Britain, *Vogue* showed a range of bizarre styles. Lobster-shaped buttons, Schiaparelli's shoe-shaped hat, a cockleshell bag of beige calf, and a 'basket ball bag' carried in a net, were obviously influenced by Dali and the Surrealists. The costume museum at Nottingham has a black suede bag, purchased at Marshall and Snelgrove's store in 1937, which is in the form of a face with applied features in black and red patent. In the following year, this bizarre tradition was continued with Schiaparelli's football-shaped bag covered in black suede 'leaves', and Molyneux's bag disguised as a leather-bound book.

With the wide-shouldered, waisted look of the late thirties, fashion saw a revival of the handbag. It appeared in a range of slightly bizarre circular, pointed or triangular shapes, in smooth materials like calf, felt or suede. In July 1938, *Vogue* recommended that a huge bag in one of the new coloured suedes be the only high note with a skirt of thin black tweed and a tailored, black suede jacket.

Since it was only in the twenties that the bag had become an integral part of a woman's outfit, and that skirts were short enough to reveal shoes, little attempt had yet been made to co-ordinate them. As British manufacturers strove to compete with the growing number of imports, however, by improving standards of design and production, there was a move to co-ordinate fashion accessories. In 1930 the British

54 *Pochette, bought in Marshall and Snelgrove in 1937. Black suede, with applied 'features' in black and red patent. Zip fastening top. Typical of the bizarre designs popularized by the Surrealist school of art in the late 1930s. (42 x 27cm.)*

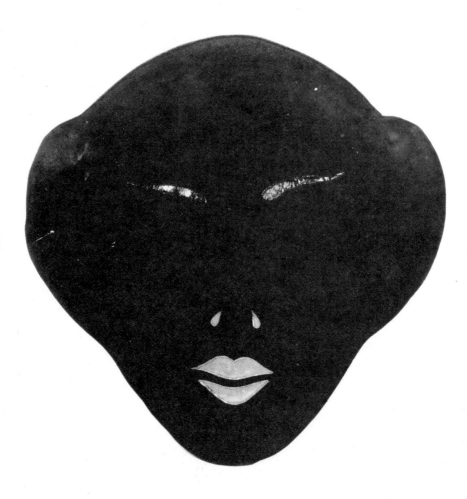

5 Knotting bag, possibly home-made, 1780-1800. White silk satin embroidered with silk and tamboured with spangles, in the light trailing patterns typical of the late 18th century. Intended to contain a knotting shuttle and thread, but probably used for fan and handkerchief, too. (29 x 24cm.)

6 Tobacco pouch and purses, 19th century. *Top left*, drawstring tobacco pouch crocheted in silk, kid-lined, 1850-70. *Next to it*, crown purse of silk and metal mesh with gilt frame and chain, late 19th century. *Below left*, jug purse of knitted green silk, gilt beads and tassel, mid-19th century. *Next to it*, bar purse of crocheted silk with steel beads and trimmings, mid-19th century. The long purses are, *from the top*, red watered silk in vandyck points, gilt metal braid and trimmings 1820-30; beige netted silk with steel beads and trimmings 1800-1810; two beadwork featuring roses, gilt metal trimmings 1820-50; green netted and beaded silk with covered sliders, probably late 19th century, but used for Bridge in the 1920s; and navy crocheted silk with steel beads and trimmings 1840-70. (Length 32cm.)

7 Evening bag, French, 1920-25. Green velvet embroidered with glass beads, and lined with flower-printed cotton. Imitation ivory frame, with press-button catch, moulded with oriental figures and stamped 'Made in France'.

8 Evening handbag, c.1934. Velvet, decorated with applied work in corded rayon, and with embroidery using silk thread and moulded glass beads, in a flower garden design typical of the 1930s. Elaborate gilt metal frame painted with flowers. (15.25 x 19cm.)

9 Day bag by Clive Shilton, 1979-80. Flower bag in soft kidskin, each 'petal' piped, gathered, and hand-finished. Clive Shilton takes the finest Italian leathers and treats them like fabric, gathering, pleating and quilting them into inventive shapes, producing luxury objects which are 'good enough to eat'.

Colour Council was set up with the specific aim of standardizing colour in British industry. Within a few years they were issuing seasonal shade cards to manufacturers, and in 1935, one began to find matching fabrics, gloves, shoes and handbags all in up-to-the-minute colours like 'Deauville beige' and 'Biarritz blue'. The year 1937 produced a sunburst of fashion colours, led by Schiaparelli's shocking pink, and mixing and matching them became a new art. In the following year, *Vogue's* 'Shophound' declared 'matched up accessories are a short cut to chic', although she had to admit that 'really nice ones are hard to come by'. By 1939, however, bags in silk or suede could be matched to gloves and shoes in the latest fashion colours of green or wine.

Travel and cosmetics continued to exert a strong influence on design. From the late twenties, holidays in the south of France or cruising in the Mediterranean had made the suntan a new status symbol, and nothing showed it off to better advantage than a pale summer dress and white accessories. Bags in linen and straw were popular, but, like leather, were difficult to clean. A popular substitute was found in Rexine, a nitro-cellulose coated cloth which had been used for document cases since before the war. Being washable, it was ideal for summer bags, from which 'even ink or lipstick can be removed'[12], and it could be embossed in a variety of textures. Thus in 1935, the Army and Navy Stores featured it in white bags of 'Spongeable Imitation Panama Straw', trimmed with red and blue morocco, at 5 shillings each.

Travel bags were increasingly sophisticated. In 1936 the Army and Navy Stores advertised wallets with special pockets for rail ticket, luggage check and bank notes, and a section covered with transparent plastic 'glazeline' to show the passport.

Encouraged by the glamour of Hollywood, cosmetics developed rapidly. One survey calculated that in 1931, fifteen hundred lipsticks were sold for every one sold ten years before. Certainly many a moiré silk or rayon bag lining at this time contains not only a flat pocket for a mirror, but a narrow lipstick pocket as well.

Naturally, vanity bags became increasingly sophisticated. By 1935, a morocco handbag with a straightforward top opening and framed inner purse might also let down at the side, revealing a fitted cigarette case, vanity case and mirror. In the late thirties many of the major cosmetic companies were producing their own fitted vanity bags 'for smart girls who have to carry round a whole day's equipment and still like their bags to keep a slim and attractive outline'.[13] Harriet Hubbard Ayer's 'Campus Carryall' was a crocodile bag with a similar side opening and a range of fitted bottles, powders, creams, lipsticks, rouge and a manicure set, while Valrosa bags, in calf or pigskin, had the addition of a separate, rubber-lined toilet bag for 'running repairs'.[14]

For the dressiest occasions, embroideries, brocades, and Viennese petit point, set on jewelled frames, were popular throughout the decade, while some of the most exciting French bags featured exquisite embroideries using a wealth of inventive beads and spangles.

Typical examples from the early thirties included designs of Chinese flowers, Eastern birds, sun rays, yachts, African goats, and lightning flashes (while, from the mid-thirties at least, English designers added a homely cottage garden scene). Worked on rich silk or gold tissue, the range and variety of the beads has probably never been matched, before or since. Porcelain and glass were moulded in individual flower shapes, with tiny veined petals; small plaques and medallions were made of painted or inlaid wood; and in the most adventurous examples, Celluloid, Galalith and other new plastics were moulded in naturalistic plant forms or cut in geometric shapes, which were applied one on top of the other to produce three-dimensional patterns.

The more bizarre taste of the late thirties produced designs in which an entire bag might be shaped like a butterfly, or patterned to look like a fish tank, with applied plastic shells and weeds, and a fish-shaped clasp.

FROM GASMASK BAGS TO AIRLINE BAGS

On the eve of the Second World War, the most popular bags were large pochettes or small framed 'dumpy bags' in suede or calf, but one result of the war was to bring a new type of bag on the market.

In 1939, as a precaution against gas attacks, 38 million gasmasks were distributed to the civilian population, to be carried night and day by every man, woman and child. Although issued in cardboard boxes, manufacturers were quick to offer special gasmask bags and cases. For Christmas 1939, Debenham and Freebody advertised a 'dainty cylinder gasmask case in velvet or corded silk', for 12 shillings 6 pence, or a combined bag and gasmask case in calf on a strong gilt frame, for 49 shillings and 6 pence. Cheaper, more practical versions appeared in Rexine or canvas, in a range of colours, so that women could match them to different outfits. The Gallery of English Costume has one in striped wool to match a smart tailored dress and jacket, and another of yellow brocade for evening wear.

55 Original bag design, French, 1938. From La
Maison Lallement, a leading couture embroidery
house, 1898-1950, the details and costings for a bag
of white satin with applied flowers and a plastic ball
sliding clasp. The sample shows petals of blue and
white plastic with yellow celluloid centres, on leaves
of ruched green ribbon and green embroidered knots.

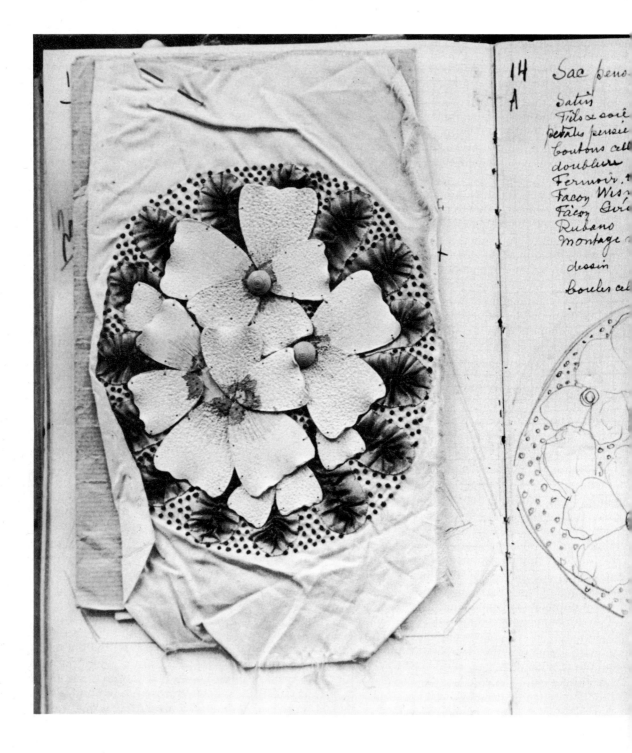

These were all supplied with long shoulder straps, as were the bags issued to the women's services, and for the duration of the war, their practicality and their military associations made shoulder bags fashionable civilian wear.

Otherwise, fashions remained static, for although handbags were never subject to rationing, the shortage of leathers and metal fittings made them increasingly expensive. (A calf bag from Marshall and Snelgrove, bought for about £2 in 1938 might cost as much as £7 in 1945.)

The only solution was 'Make Do and Mend', and in 1943, *Vogue* advised saving leather by making bags from old remnants of satin or felt, a good substitute for suede. A simple flat envelope pochette was easy to make, and could be dressed up for evenings with the addition of a jewelled clip or brooch. The favourite style, however, was the gathered pouch bag made from a simple rectangle of fabric folded in two, seamed at the bottom and half way up the sides, and gathered by a fabric ring in the middle, leaving a loop at the top which was slung over the wrist. (This style proved so popular that it was made commercially after the war.)

With the end of the war, *Vogue's* 'Demobilization Wardrobe' for 1945 was based on simplicity, and readers were advised to 'choose large, important bags and good shoes and gloves'. Stocks could not be replenished overnight, however. Leather was still in short supply, as were tapes for zip fasteners, and double-sided handbag mirrors were banned while glass was still needed to replace bomb-shattered windows. Rationing was still in force, and with the bad harvests of 1945, food shortages were worse than ever. A new handbag could only be thought of as a special gift. The really essential container was the shopping bag, for 'Everyone carried a shopping bag in case they should be lucky enough to pass a shop that had a sudden stock of something off the rations'.[15]

As the situation improved in the late forties and early fifties, however, women completely rejected the shoulder bags and home-made pochettes of wartime, turning instead to professionally manufactured, boxy handbags in trunk, cylinder or hat-box shapes, on thick metal frames. Many were made in leather, which was becoming more readily available, but in 1948, among the government's fiscal measures aimed at putting the country back on its feet, leather goods received a purchase tax of 100 per cent. Although this was lowered in 1952, it gave an additional impetus to a new leather substitute.

This was Vynide, a fabric coated with polyvinyl chloride, already being used by Morris Motors for car upholstery. It was hard-wearing, light, and washable, and could be impressed with any texture. In 1948, Woollands offered a white Vynide bag in imitation morocco at 45 shillings 1 penny, and in the follow-

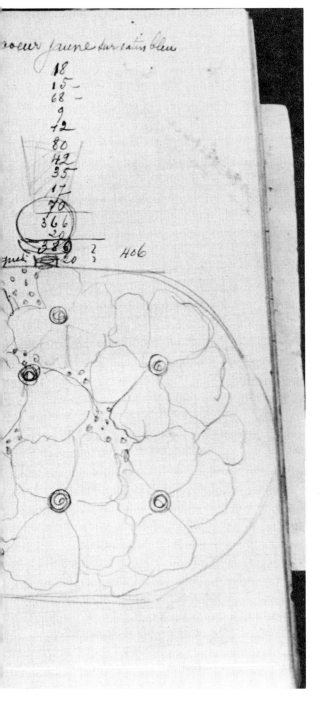

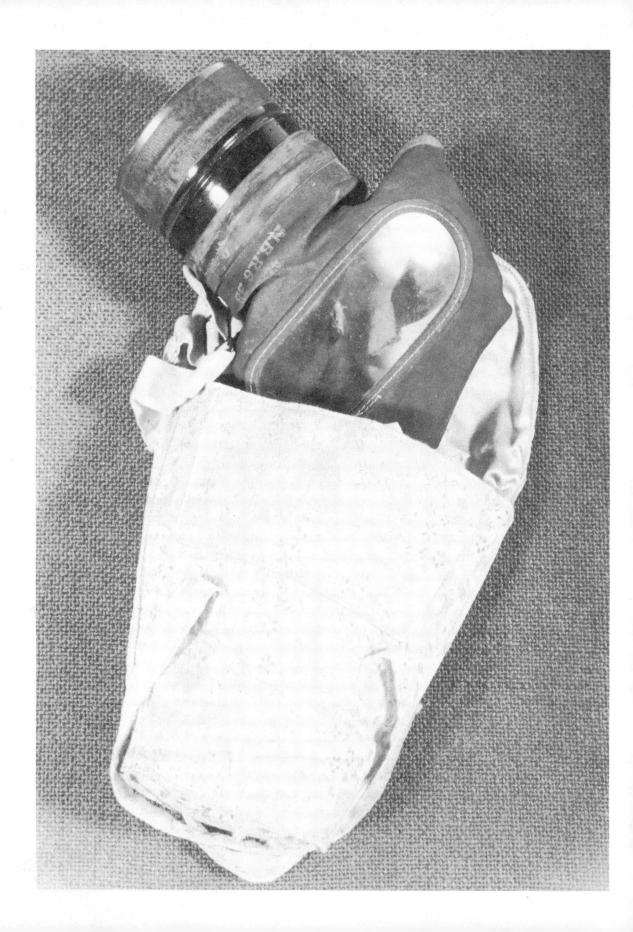

ing year, *Vogue* welcomed lizard-grained Vynide with the comment that 'Plastic bags have improved beyond recognition, so better a good plastic than a poor leather'.

During the 1950s, plastics were to go from strength to strength, fulfilling a need for cheap, light bags in a range of colours that included the washable whites and pastels to match new easy-care man-made fabrics. By the early fifties, expensive skins could all be substituted by PVC cloths like Lizadex, Crocadex or even Emudex, while piping and handles appeared in extruded PVC, Xylonite, and Polystyrene. With the

56 *Evening gasmask bag, with gasmask, 1938-45. Cream twilled cotton and man-made fibre, figured in yellow viscose rayon with a pattern of gazelles, panthers, and flowers. Short carrying handles. Bought for party wear, although never actually used. (Height 20cm.)*

57 *Plastic handbag, American, c.1955. Clear plastic, decorated with pink plastic shells. Handle and frame of stiffened white kid. Bought from Saks of Fifth Avenue, and used by Dame Alicia Markova. The United States led the way in the development and use of plastics during and after the Second World War.*

58 Cartoon by Adamson, from Punch, 1955. The open-topped bucket bag was at its most popular in this year.

Adamson

growing popularity of linen and Italian straws for summer, PVC was impressed with straw and fabric textures, and in the late fifties, the fashion for smoother leathers was copied in artificial patent, or plastic padded with foam to give the supple effect of baby calf.

The predominant theme of the 1950s was the 'good handbag', chosen not for its individuality but for its ability to match the shoes and the dress or suit. Top-fastening bags were the most usual, with frames of steel or lacquered brass, and the angular pencil-line skirts of the early fifties favoured slim, angular bags, made neat by flaps and suitcase fastenings, or concealed leather-covered frames. Pochettes reap-

peared as 'clutch bags', and might be carried with flared 'dustcoats' by day, or with full-skirted taffeta gowns by night. In 1954, *Vogue* recommended 'definite outlines, unfussy shapes' in 'soft, softest antelope' or hide, and welcomed the 'new clear line' of a thin melon-wedge clutch bag in polished calf, by Bembaron. A narrow rectangular clutch bag was the favourite accessory with Dior's A-line of 1955, and was to remain popular with young or 'dainty' styles until well into the 1960s.

New versions of the war-time shopping bag were an alternative to the handbag, and remained exempt from purchase tax, provided that they were open at the top. The stiffened 'bucket' shape, introduced from France, was popular throughout the decade, and paved the way for larger and larger handbags after 1955. Many of these were in the same expansive shape, capable of carrying the office girl's lunch, magazines, and cosmetics — 'The last, late typists, their bucket bags stuffed with deodorants and paper handkerchiefs . . . .'[16] Smarter bags appeared in the form of large flat envelopes, with or without handles, like Jane Shilton's 'big brief case bag' of 1958 'with square gilt locks'.[17]

For the smart woman, strict rules of accessorizing were laid down in a regular *Vogue* feature called 'What to wear with what'. Colour co-ordination was the main theme, and a typical chart of 1952 showed twenty-five diffferent colour schemes for dresses and accessories. The favourite bag colours were cream, brown, pewter, or navy, but a cream dress might have a blue hat, white gloves, and matching shoes and bag in 'vin rosé'. As the decade progressed, white and pastel shades like lilac, 'heavenly blue', and 'Japonica', grew increasingly popular, especially with the young.

For travelling or shopping, there were also Italian straw baskets and ladies' brief-cases, and, in the early fifties, airlines were producing a new status symbol in the multi-coloured overnight bags of PVC or canvas, which were given free to long-flight passengers, or could be purchased by short-flight passengers for about 15 shillings.

59 Handbags, 1950-70. Back, bucket-type bag in brown plastic, 1950-60. (Depth 29cm.) Right, afternoon bag in chocolate brown grosgrain with covered brass frame, 1950-55. Front, day bag of white painted metal plaques. White plastic frame and chain. Lining of black taffeta, 1965-70. Right, evening bag of lacquered brass, covered with black ribbed silk. The front lets down to reveal a gathered pocket and large fitted mirror, 1950.

For afternoon visits and Bridge, or early evening cocktails, there were smaller bags of pleated grosgrain, or, by 1956, smooth leathers like the antelope with mother-of-pearl frame, advertised by Fior. For evening, there were matching shoes and bags in rich brocades, while petit point, gold and silver kid, and diamanté clutch bags were also popular.

In 1952, a woman who complained that tiny evening bags would not hold both cosmetics and cigarette case, was told that 'any woman smart enough to carry this tiny handbag is sure of an escort who will provide the cigarettes'[18], but some manufacturers recognized the dilemma, and produced special party bags. Thus in 1955, a Stratton silk evening bag, fitted with gilt compact, lipstick and cigarette case, could be bought for £4 10 shillings.

Manufacturers were aware of the younger market throughout the 1950s. From 1953, the shoulder bag was revived in the form of a flapped and buckled 'sling bag' in coach hide or English pigskin, to be worn with country tweeds, or with the more casual styles of the twenties' age group. The cheaper plastic handbags in pastel colours were also favoured by the young, and the clutch bag was seen as suitably 'dainty' for the teenager. By 1960, however, the post-war bulge had made the teenage market large enough to be worth cultivating in its own right. Casual drawstring 'duffle bags' appeared, decorated with rock'n roll motifs, and bag manufacturers launched a nationwide television campaign to promote a new 'student bag' — an updated version of the brief-case. The prophetic slogan in *Leathergoods* in 1960 was 'Tempt the teenager — it's a profitable business'.

---

60 *Evening clutch bag, 1960. A 'melon-wedge' shaped, flapped bag of pink satin, with satin piping and diamanté trimming. Made by Delman, and worn with matching evening shoes by Rayne. Typical of the 'dainty' styles in sugar colours popular around 1960.*

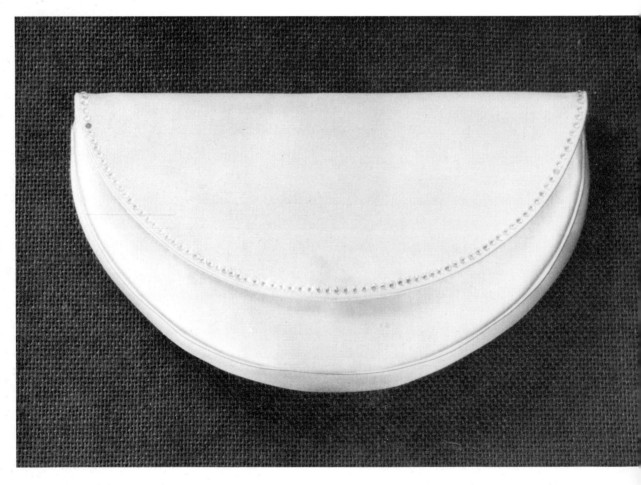

FROM DOLLY BAGS TO SOFTBAGS

The fashions of the 1960s were to be dominated by the teenage market, and although manufacturers continued to produce more conservative styles for those women who were not leggy teenagers (or could not pretend to be), the main trends in styling were set by the young. The startling changes in their clothing fashions required bag manufacturers to have a greater awareness of the latest fashion trends, and it was often from outsiders, like the actress Sally Jess, with her bags for trouser suits, that new concepts in design were first introduced.

In 1961, teenage girls were still wearing shirt-waister dresses and stiletto heels, and carrying PVC clutch bags in 'pastel pink' or 'pearlized peppermint'. By 1962, however, Chanel's casual 'sling bag' of black patent, on a chunky gilt chain, was becoming popular with all age groups, and teenage readers of *Honey* magazine were advised to make their own, using cheap chains from the costume jewellery counters. In the same year, a vogue for shiny PVC mackintoshes

and wellington boots, in bright red or black, confirmed glossy PVC patent bags as a fashion for the young, and these were suitably bright and casual with the shorter skirts and 'fun' clothes of 1963. As models danced and jumped their way across the pages of young magazines, they set quilted patent shoulder bags swinging in true sixties' style.

In 1965, under the influence of St Laurent's Op Art black and white shifts, and Courrèges' sculptural white minis of the previous year, coloured patents were rivalled by stark black and white bags in flat angular shapes. For wear with a Courrèges-style dress, *Honey* showed a flat home-made bag, consisting of a folded rectangle of white fabric, seamed at bottom and sides, with the two upper corners cut

---

61 Convertible shoulder bag, 1966. Triple bag, small enough to be carried as a handbag with mini skirts, but with an adjustable strap on 'dog-leash' clips, for wear with trouser suits.

away to leave a handle.

As mini skirts shortened, framed handbags grew smaller, becoming wafer thin and streamlined, with concealed clasps, zip fastenings, or even side openings. In 1966, flat bags with hard rectangular cut-out handles reflected the cut-outs on Courrèges boots, while small bags made of large white plastic beads were in the mood of Paco Rabanne's plastic disc dresses.

As trouser suits became a popular alternative to the mini skirt, there was a demand for more informal styles of handbag that were less obviously feminine. One answer was Sally Jess's flat, unstructured, rectangular bags, slung from straight plastic bar handles. Alternatively, the shoulder bag was suited to the longer line of the trouser suit, and many manufacturers already producing tiny 'Dolly' handbags for the mini skirt, added separate shoulder straps (attached by dog-leash clips) for use with trousers.

To maintain the look of a tiny bag, while still allowing room for all the paraphernalia of cigarettes, tickets, cheque book, tissues, false eyelashes and assorted cosmetics carried by the sixties' teenager, double-sided bags were introduced, followed by bags with rows of outside pockets, with flap and buckle fastenings. These had the advantage of looking business-like with trousers, and in the same vein, multi-pocketed 'Doctor' bags, and smaller versions of the 'Gladstone bag' (so popular with male travellers in the nineteenth century) had suitably masculine overtones. Equally practical was the huge 'tote bag' with its separate cosmetic bag compartment and photograph pockets, as used by that idol of the sixties, the model girl.

In 1966, Op Art colours produced bags in purple, scarlet, 'Pacific blue', or 'Samoa yellow', worn with outfits in startling colour combinations, and this was followed, in 1967, by a rainbow of psychedelic colours and flower motifs. These were popularized in the large paper tote bags printed in Art Nouveau swirls of yellow, shocking pink and orange, or green, turquoise and lilac. Costing only 9 pence or 1 shilling, they were cheap, roomy, and unisex, and printed in the newest pattern and colourway they were an instant link with the latest fashion trends. (Printed PVC soon provided a more substantial, and only slightly more expensive alternative.)

In 1969, 'wet-look bags' had ICI's new glossy polyurethane coating, which was more hardwearing and flexible than PVC. Flap-over bags in this fabric were soft and squashy, and trimmed with large circular buckles they were soon popular alternatives to 'mock croc', 'fake snake', and shiny patent.

Traditional styles were still being produced throughout the sixties, of course, as they are today. In evening bags, a new aluminium and nylon weave mesh revived Edwardian-style gold and silver mesh purses, while L.W. Krucker was still importing Austrian petit point bags, and oriental embroidered fabrics, on dainty frames and metal chains. For day, Gucci's exquisitely made satchels in real leather were expensive but classic, and firms like Jane Shilton provided middle-priced, good quality handbags, brought up to date with fashionable motifs. In the more conservative styles, the bright colours of 1966 were echoed in two-tone effects of red and navy, while the swirling patterns of 1967 influenced Salisbury's to produce evening brocades in abstract shapes and squiggles.

From 1967, 'flower power' romanticism provided an alternative to minis and bright plastics. With Indian caftans and long cheesecloth skirts the only suitable styles were soft, fabric shoulder bags in Indian embroideries, or Iraqui woven cloths, trimmed with thick cords and tassels. As longer skirts and ethnic styles became high fashion, around 1970, these shoulder bags appeared everywhere in hessian, oriental carpet fabrics, and soft suedes in patchwork or multicoloured appliqués.

In 1972, the interest in the 1930s produced a range of sleeker, more tailored clothes. 'Try dressing like a lady', said *Vogue*, and with soft midi-length knitted suits and little hats, the natural accompaniment was the pochette in pastel shades of glacé kid, or the improved 'soft touch' polyurethane. In 1973, Christopher Trill produced a range of angular, woven leather pochettes, but the compromise with ethnic styles was still retained in Lesley Slight's envelope bags in pale appliquéd leathers.

The general trend, however, was towards the casual layered look, in natural fabrics. Huge shapeless sweaters and tweeds need large natural leather shoulder bags in softer styles, and the 'Hobo bag' appeared with its zip fastening top and soft crescent shape. The canvas tote bag was a practical alternative, with both trousers and skirts, and for use by both men and women, so that by 1973, retailers were

---

62 *Suede shoulder bags, 1970. In 1970 Maria and Gussy set up their own business, supplying the market for hand-made appliqué suede bags to suit the current romantic, 'ethnic' fashions. (Disc jockey Jimmy Saville bought one which he used for carrying his cigars, thus encouraging the trend towards unisex bags.)*

faced with the problem of whether to sell it as a handbag, shopping bag, or luggage.

Indeed, as plasticized fabrics made luggage increasingly light and unstructured, it came closer in style to the soft pouchy handbag. In the early seventies, inspired by Louis Vuitton's extended range of vinyl luggage, patterned with the exclusive 'LV' initials, Dior and other couture houses began producing their own ranges of initialled canvas bags. These followed the general trend for fabric bags, while maintaining the caché, and the price, of expensive leather.

As the casual layered look continued into the mid-seventies, shoulder bags became larger than ever, and by 1975, *Vogue* was choosing huge fishing bags and hunting bags to go with chunky wools and tweeds. As the credit squeeze of the sixties became the economic recession of the seventies, however, soaring prices and a world shortage made leather a luxury item. In the prevailing mood of economic gloom, the traditional leather bag seemed in bad taste. Instead, ethnic styles were revived, and Jap produced tiny fabric shoulder purses, worn diagonally across the body, with his oriental peasant clothes, while his quilted cotton jackets were echoed in a range of quilted canvas shoulder bags. Even at the top end of the market, where leather *was* in demand bags took large, soft informal shapes with a zip or flap fastening, rather than a large heavy frame. In 1976, *Vogue* showed a printed suede tote bag by Loewe which cost £119, and was worn slung casually over the shoulder in a shapeless pouch. The appeal of such bags was subtle, consisting of their exquisite soft supple leathers and perfect finishing. In this the Italians led the field, and in the same year the Italian-based firm of Enny, renowned for their 'softbags' since 1966, opened their first London outlet.

Soft roomy bags with pockets, in the Enny style, were the dominant theme of the late seventies. The swinging teenager of the sixties had grown up to be the liberated working woman of the seventies, and for her harassed and busy life, the mail order 'organizer bag' featured no less than twelve pockets to hold make-up, tissues, keys, sunglasses, cigarettes and lighter, tickets, change, cheque book, credit cards, photographs, season tickets, stamps, address books, diary, bills, and letters, all easily located with the minimum of rummaging.

Ironically, in the last years of the seventies, soaring prices in all materials have encouraged a return to real leather as an investment, although shops have had to explain the properties and natural marks to a generation accustomed to vinyl. In 1979, however, Jean Tournier provided another answer to the problem of price and durability with the introduction here of zipped 'sacs'. Made of strong, cheap parachute-grade nylon, they are the ultimate 'softbag', and their range of bright colours appeals especially to the young, both male and female.

The British have always looked to the French for stylish fashion accessories, and since the last war, luxurious Italian leather bags have also been imported in increasing numbers. By 1980, the British market was again dominated by foreign products, and even the more conservative styles were being imported from Europe and Japan, or made up abroad for British manufacturers. Bag-making is a highly labour intensive trade. Even the modern leather softbag can require up to eighty-five separate operations in its manufacture[19], and with rising prices, bag makers have turned to areas like Hong Kong and Korea where labour is cheap. South America, too, is entering the field, and capitalizing on its combination of native leathers and cheap labour.

With the growth of interest in crafts over the last decade, however, a number of bags are now being hand-made by individal craftsmen whose freedom from the limitations of mass production has enabled them to experiment with designs and materials. Naturally, high costs mean that they are catering predominantly for the luxury end of the market, but their designs and ideas have influenced larger manufacturers. Clive Shilton's quilted scallop shell bag of 1976, for example, has been widely copied at all levels, and has helped to revive the demand for exciting designs.

The last years of the seventies have seen designers experimenting with new ideas in a range of small fantasy bags. A revival of 1950s dress, complete with tailored skirts and little hats, provoked a demand for bags that were small, brightly coloured, and witty. In 1976, Christopher Trill showed a tiny duffle bag made in silver kid, and Clive Shilton produced his shell bag, first in screen-printed satin, and then in soft supple leather. By 1979, tiny bags appeared in a whole range of novel materials and shapes, from pink suede hearts to Yuki's discs of Japanese lacquer work, from Regine's wooden caskets to Malcolm Parsons' clutch bags of coloured paper. Many of these bags

63 Enny softbag, 1981. Zip-fastening shoulder bag of supple calf by the Italian firm of Enny, renowned for their softbags since the late 1960s. These light capacious bags avoid the weight and formality of the framed bag, and are ideally suited to the casual and sporty styles which emerged in the 1970s.

could be seen as decorative objects in their own right, and when a designer like Clive Shilton made up his novel shell and flower shapes in the rich colours and supple fabric of the best Italian leathers, handbags were once again a joy both to look at and to use.

'MAN BAGS'

In the nineteenth century carpet bags and Gladstone bags were used by men as overnight or business cases, and from the 1920s professional brief and attaché bags were adopted by the smart businessman for his papers. Naturally the latter have also been useful for his sandwiches and the odd paperback, but they were used primarily for business purposes.

The increase in the student population of the late fifties and sixties meant that student styles in the form of duffle, kit and airling bags, were widely used by the young, and fashionable Carnaby Street dressers added denim shoulder bags and canvas totes. In the sixties, too, photographers' equipment bags had the same caché for young men as the model-girl totes for women. These styles were virtually exlusive to the young and 'trendy', however. Most men continued to rely on pockets to hold their money and personal belongings, and regarded bags as effeminate.

From the late fifties, however, the growing popularity of the two-piece suit in light man-made fibres encouraged slimmer and better-fitting clothes in which well-filled pockets looked unsightly. This did not deter the Englishman from filling them, but in countries like Italy, where fashion-conscious men wore slim, pocketless shirts and trousers, even when they discarded jackets for hot summer wear, an alternative was found in leather shoulder bags or wrist bags.

With the growth of tourism, too, the multi-pocketed camera bag and general touring bag, on convenient shoulder straps, were proving popular accessories with the Americans, Germans and Japanese. As the Englishman took more foreign holidays and business trips, he gradually became acclimatized to these 'man bags', and began to use them himself, at least when abroad.

By 1971, the English leather goods' journals were beginning to discuss the potential market for these styles. The general attitude was summed up by one retailer in *Leathergoods* of that year, who declared 'The man-bag? No self-respecting Englishman would be seen with one!', but proceeded to stock one or two just in case.

Over the last decade, demand has grown steadily, and in 1974 Bryan Forbes struck a blow for 'Men's Lib' at the Antiquarian Book Fair, when he refused to allow his canvas shoulder bag to be searched by security men when women's handbags were exempt. By 1979, multi-pocketed bags for men were available in soft Italian calf, solid German hide, or a range of leathers and vinyls imported from Japan. Both shoulder bags and smaller wrist bags with a wrist loop were available at most shops which stocked luggage, menswear or women's handbags, and were so similar to the better 'organizer' bags that many women were buying them too.

As society becomes increasingly sophisticated, and demands that we carry more clutter in the way of identity cards, credit cards, tickets for public services, etc., men may once again prefer the bag to the pocket, and with the growing popularity of brightly coloured, all-purpose, nylon 'sacs', the bag may once more become both decorative and unisex.

Notes

CHAPTER 1

FROM POUCHES TO POCKETS
1 Illustrated in J. Waterer, *Leather Craftsmanship*, G. Bell and Sons, 1968, Pl. 61.
2 W. Shakespeare, *As You Like It*, 1600, II, vii, 158.
3 R. Holme, *Academy of Armory*, Chester, 1688, Vol. II, p. 336.
4 T. Coryate, *Coryat's . . . Crudities*, 1611, p. 66.
5 E. (Ned) Ward, *The London Spy*, 1698-1700, edited by A.L. Hayward, Cassell, 1927, p. 224.
6 From R. Hackluyt, quoted in E. Partridge, *A Dictionary of Slang*, Routledge & Kegan Paul, 1974, Vol. I, p. 26.
7 John and Mary Evelyn, *Mundus Muliebris 1690*, edited by J.L. Nevinson, Costume Society, 1977, p. 11.
8 I am indebted to Miss Janet Arnold for this information on the gown at Bath, and for notes on the inventories of Queen Elizabeth I which are to be published in her forthcoming book *Queen Elizabeth's Wardrobe Unlock'd*.

TIE POCKETS
9 Iona and Peter Opie, *The Oxford Dictionary of Nursery Rhymes*, Oxford University Press, 1951, p. 279.
10 Lady F.P. Verney, *Memoirs of the Verney Family*, edited by M. Verney, Longmans, Green & Co., 1904, 24 November 1650, Vol. I, p. 469.
11 A.M. Earle, *Two Centuries of Costume in America, 1620-1820*, 1903, reprinted Dover, 1970, Vol. II, p. 586.
12 Quoted in C.W. and P. Cunnington, *Handbook of English Costume in the Eighteenth Century*, Faber & Faber, 1972 ed. p. 339.
13 The Ambrose Heal Collection of Trade Cards, British Museum.
14 Quoted in T. Hughes, *English Domestic Needlework*, Lutterworth Press, 1961, p. 244.
15 A.M. Earle, *op. cit.*, p. 589.

16 T. Smollett, *Humphrey Clinker*, 1771, Oxford University Press, 1967, p. 111.

SEVENTEENTH-CENTURY SWEET BAGS AND PURSES
17 Lord William Howard of Naworth Castle, 'The Household Books of', *Surtees Society* Publication No. 68, Durham, 1878, p. 256.
18 S. Rowlands, *Dr Merry-Man*, 1607, quoted in C.W. & P. Cunnington, *Handbook of English Costume in the Seventeenth Century*, Faber, 1972 ed., p. 77 (Cunnington quotes 1616 edition).
19 R. Greene, 'Second Part of Cony-Catching' 1591, edited by A.V. Judges in *The Elizabethan Underworld*, G. Routledge & Sons, 1930, p. 167.
20 S. Rowlands, 'Greene's Ghost', 1602, quoted in C.W. & P. Cunnington, *op. cit.*, p. 78.
21 R. Greene, 'Third Part of Cony-Catching', 1592, A.V. Judges, *op. cit.*, p. 203.
22 *Ibid.*, p. 189.
23 *Ibid.*, p. 195
24 John and Mary Evelyn, *op. cit.*, p. 4
25 G. Scott Thomson, *Life in a Noble Household 1641-1700*, Jonathan Cape, 1937, p. 344.
26 Henry Howard, Earl of Northampton, 'Inventory of the Effects of . . .', 1614, *Archaeologia*, XLII, Vol. II, pp. 347-78.
27 Lady F.P. Verney, *op. cit.*, 12 November 1639, Vol. II, p. 154.
28 John and Mary Evelyn, *op. cit.*, p. 11.
29 Ben Jonson, 'The Masque of Queens', 1609, in *Works*, W. Bulmer, London, 1816, Vol. 7, p. 131.

'THE GIFT OF A FRIEND'
30 J. Nichols, *The Progresses of Elizabeth I*, London, 1823, Vol. I, p. XL, note i.
32 J. Nichols, *The Progresses of James I*, London, 1828, Vol. II, p. 644 & Vol. III, p. 270.
33 Sir John Harington, 'The Letters and Epigrams of . . . ', ed. N.E. McClure, University of Pennsylvania Press, 1930, p. 95.
34 John Evelyn, *Tyrannus or the Mode*, 1661, quoted in C.W. & P. Cunnington, *op. cit.*, p. 152.

35 J. Parkinson, *Paradisi in sole Paradisus Terrestris*, 1629, p. 116.

EIGHTEENTH-CENTURY PURSES
36 T. Smollett, *op. cit.*, p. 429.
37 Quoted in S. Groves, *The History of Needlework Tools and Accessories*, Country Life, 1966, p. 108.
38 *Ibid.*
39 D. Diderot, *L'Encyclopédie, ou Dictionnaire Raisonné des Sciences, des Arts et des Métiers* 1751, Vol. I.
40 Ambrose Heal coll., *op. cit.*
41 Larry Salmon, 'Ballooning: Accessories after the Fact' in *Dress*, the Journal of the Costume Society of America, Vol. II, 1976 No. 1, pp. 1-9.
42 Banks Collection of Trade Cards, British Museum.
43 C. Hutton, *Reminiscences of a Gentlewoman of the Last Century*, edited by Mrs C.H. Beale, 1891, pp. 54, 213.
44 Ambrose Heal coll., *op. cit.*
45 W. M. Thackeray, *Vanity Fair*, London, 1847-8, Ch. 4.

THE PURSE TRADE
46 Lord Howard of Naworth, *op. cit.*, p. 75.
47 Ambrose Heal coll., *op. cit.*
48 Rev. J. Woodforde, *Diary of a Country Parson 1758-1802*, edited by J. Beresford, Oxford Univeristy Press, 1979 ed., p. 437.
49 Ambrose Heal coll., *op. cit.*
50 Banks coll., *op. cit.*

LETTER CASES AND POCKET BOOKS
51 Illustrated in Seligman, G. and Hughes, T., *Domestic Needlework*, Country Life, 1926.
52 H. Fielding, *Tom Jones*, 1749, Book XII, Ch. 4.
53 T. Smollett, *Roderick Random*, 1748.
54 G. Reynolds, *Samuel Cooper's Pocket Book*, Victoria and Albert Museum Brochure, 1975.
55 Mrs Delany, *The Autobiography and Correspondence*, edited by Lady Llanover, 1861-2, 2 January 1772, Series 2, Vol. I, p. 399.
56 E. Purefoy, *Purefoy Letters 1735-53*, edited by G. Eland, Sidgwick & Jackson, 1931, 13 June 1741, Vol. II, p. 252.
57 Mrs Delany, *op. cit.*, Series 2, Vol. II, December 1779, p. 496.
58 W. Hone, *The Table Book*, 1828, Vol. II, p. 403.

FROM WORK BAGS TO RETICULES
59 Ambrose Heal coll., *op. cit.* (A housewife is a type of needlecase.)
60 Lady Mary Coke, *Letters and Journals*, Kingsmere Reprints, Bath, 1970, 26-27 October 1769,

Vol. III, p. 162.
61 Lady Louisa Stuart, 1798, quoted in N. Waugh, *The Cut of Women's Clothes 1600-1930*, Faber & Faber, 1968, p. 211.

CHAPTER 2

INVENTIVE RETICULES
1 Quoted in C.W. Cunnington, *Englishwomen's Clothing in the Nineteenth Century*, Faber, 1937, p. 73.
2 T. Hope, *Designs of Modern Costume*, 1812, edited by J.L. Nevinson, Costume Society reprint.
3 A.M. Earle, *op. cit.*, Vol. II, p. 594.

CHATELAINES AND CHATELAINE BAGS
4 See article in the *Englishwoman's Domestic Magazine*, 1875.
5 Lady Viola Greville, *The Gentlewoman in Society*, Henry & Co., London, 1892, p. 251.

FROM CARRIAGE BAGS TO HAND BAGS
6 Oscar Wilde, *The Importance of Being Earnest*, 1899, Act Three.
7 See *Queen* magazine, 1868, p. 436.
8 S. Druitt, *Antique Personal Possessions*, Blandford Press, Poole, 1980, p. 52.

MORE PURSES AND POCKET BOOKS
9 J. Austen, *Pride and Prejudice*, 1813, Ch. VIII.

CHAPTER 3

PURSE BAGS AND DOROTHY BAGS
1 *The Bag, Portmanteau and Umbrella Trader*, 1907.
2 Quoted in E. Ewing, *History of 20th Century Fashion*, B.T. Batsford, 1974, p. 75.
3 *Ibid.*
4 *The Bag, Portmanteau and Umbrella Trader*, 1907-8.
5 *Ibid.*, 1909.
6 *Ibid.*, 1910.
7 S. Druitt, *op. cit.*, pp. 54, 57.

PLASTICS AND POCHETTES
8 *The Bag, Portmanteau and Umbrella Trader*, 1920.
9 *Ibid.*, 1916.
10 M. Arlen, *The Green Hat*, W. Collins and Sons, 1924, p. 16.
11 *The Bag, Portmanteau and Umbrella Trader*, 1920.

CRUISE BAGS AND BEADS
12 *The Fancy Goods Trader*, 1935.
13 *Vogue*, 1938.
14 *Ibid.*

FROM GASMASK BAGS TO AIRLINE BAGS
15 M. Spark, *The Girls of Slender Means*, 1963, Penguin Books ed., 1980, p. 9.

16 K. Waterhouse, *Billy Liar*, 1959, Penguin edition, 1980, p. 20.
17 *Vogue*, 1958.
18 *Leathergoods*, 1952.

FROM DOLLY BAGS TO SOFTBAGS
19 M. Cahn, *The Factory* (a portrait of the Coach leathergoods factory), New York, 1977.

Bibliography

Bayerische Versicherungskammer, Munich, *Modisches aus alter Zeit: Accessoires vier Jahrhunderten*, (exhibition catalogue) 1979.

British Industrial Plastics Ltd, *Plastic Antiques* (the catalogue to the exhibition of that name first shown at Wolverhampton Polytechnic in 1977).

Buck, A., *Victorian Costume and Costume Accessories*, Herbert Jenkins, 1961.

Cunnington, C.W., *English Women's Clothing in the Nineteenth Century*, Faber and Faber, 1937.
English Women's Clothing in the Present Century, Faber and Faber, 1952.

Cunnington, C.W. & P., *Handbook of English Costume in the Seventeenth Century*, Faber, 1955.
Handbook of English Costume in the Eighteenth Century, Faber, 1957.

D'Allemagne, H.R. *Les Accessoires du Costume*, 3 Vols, Schemit, 1928.

Diderot, D., *L'Encyclopédie, ou Dictionnaire Raisonné des Sciences, des Arts et des Métiers*, 1751.

Dibgy, G.W., *Elizabethan Embroidery*, Faber and Faber, 1963.

Double, W.C., *Design and Construction of Handbags*, Oxford, 1960.

Druitt, Silvia, *Antique Personal Possessions*, Blandford Press, 1980.

Earle, A.M., *Two Centuries of Costume in America (1620-1820)*, 2 Vols., 1903, reprinted by Dover, 1970.

Groves, Sylvia, *The History of Needlework Tools and Accessories*, Country Life, 1966.

Hughes, T., *English Domestic Needlework, 1660-1860*, Lutterworth Press, 1961.

Morris, B., *Victorian Embroidery*, Herbert Jenkins, 1962.

Nevinson, J.L., *Catalogue of English Domestic Embroidery of the 16th and 17th Centuries*, Victoria and Albert Museum, 1938.

Salmon, L., 'Ballooning: accessories after the fact', in *Dress*, the Journal of the Costume Society of America, Vol. II, 1976, no. 1.

Schoeffler, O.E. and Gale, W., *Esquire's Encyclopedia of 20th Century Men's Fashions*, McGraw-Hill, New York, 1973.

Seligman, G., and Hughes, T., *Domestic Needlework*, Country Life, 1926.

Waterer, J.W., *Leather: in Life, Art & Industry*, Faber, 1946.
Leather Craftsmanship, G. Bell & Sons, 1968.

The Workman's Guide, by 'A Lady', 1838, new edition 1840, reprinted by Bloomfield Books, 1975.

TRADE CATALOGUES AND JOURNALS
A. Adburgham (intro.) *Victorian Shopping*, the Harrods' Stores Catalogue, 1895, reprinted by David & Charles, 1972.
Yesterday's Shopping, the Army & Navy Stores Catalogue, 1907, reprinted by David & Charles, 1969.

Ackermann's *Repository of Arts*
The *Englishwoman's Domestic Magazine*
Queen
The Lady's Newspaper
The Bag, Portmanteau, and Umbrella Trader, and Fancy Leather Goods and Athletic Trades Review.
The Fancy Goods Record
The Fancy Goods Trader
Leathergoods
Vogue
Honey
Assorted Trade Catalogues in the Museum of London.

Glossary

of Materials and Decorative Techniques (not explained in the text).

Bakelite phenol-formaldehyde resin, the first synthetic plastic. Developed in the USA.

Berlin woolwork embroidery in worsteds, mainly in tent or cross stitch on canvas, the designs copied stitch by stitch from printed patterns. In the nineteenth century Berlin was the main centre for the production of these patterns, and for the dyeing of the wools.

Bobbin lace openwork mesh fabric made on a lace pillow, by twisting and interweaving threads wound on bobbins.

Brocade a woven silk, with elaborate patterns created by the introduction of additional threads of coloured silk or metal.

Buckram a coarse, plain-weave linen fabric, stiffened with size.

Buttonhole stitch (or blanket stitch) a vertical stitch linked to its neighbour by a horizontal stitch at the base. A second row can be worked from the horizontal stitches of the first row, and so built up to create a mesh fabric which is the basis of needlepoint lace.

Calf leather made from the skin of young cattle, and characterized by a smooth finish.

Calico a plain-weave cotton cloth, coarser than muslin.

Cambric in the seventeenth century, a fine, plain-weave linen cloth, but in the nineteenth century the term was also applied to fine cottons.

Chenille a silk thread with a long pile, making it look like a furred caterpillar.

Coach hide a thick, smooth leather made from cattle hide, which has been vegetable-tanned, dyed and matt-finished.

Crewel work embroidery using coloured worsteds on a tough linen and cotton fabric. Stylized oriental plant patterns were worked in this technique on curtains and bed-hangings in the late seventeenth century.

Dimity a strong twilled fabric with a linen warp and cotton weft. Often woven with a distinctive rib.

Flamestitch embroidery (also called florentine or bargello work) rows of vertical stitches worked on canvas in zig zag lines of gradated colours to produce a flame-like pattern.

French knots embroidered bead-like knots, produced by winding the thread twice around the needle before completing the stitch.

Fustian a fabric with a linen warp and a cotton weft.

Gimp a thick cord, thread or braid.

Gobelin stitch horizontal rows of tent stitches, but worked over *two* warp and one weft threads, and interlocking with the row above to produce a slightly openwork ground.

Grosgrain a plain-weave fabric, usually silk or artificial silk, with prominent horizontal ribs.

Gunmetal a dull grey metal, an alloy of copper and tin or zinc, once used for guns.

Laid and couched work in embroidery, large stitches or cords of thick silk or metal thread laid across the fabric and caught down or 'couched' at intervals by smaller stitches.

Lizard the scaly skin of Indian or Javan lizards, sometimes dyed, but in its natural state coloured in shades of fawn or grey.

Moiré a ribbed silk or artificial silk with a watered pattern produced by flattening areas of ribbing with heated rollers.

Morocco originally a goatskin tanned with sumach and given a characteristic pebble pattern by 'boarding', i.e. folding and creasing. Later, the term might be applied to inferior skins embossed with a 'morocco' pattern.

Needlepoint lace (*see* Buttonhole stitch)

Paillettes the French word for 'spangle', and used by embroiderers to describe types of large and variously shaped spangle.

Patent originally a hide coated with layers of varnish or lacquer to produce a hard gloss, but now often imitated by plasticized nitro-cellulose or synthetic resins.

Petit point (*see* Tent stitch).

Pinchbeck an alloy of copper and zinc made to imitate gold, and, in England, developed by Christopher Pinchbeck.

Plush a silk or cotton fabric with a long pile.

Polyurethane (PU) a synthetic plastic, now developed as a resin coating for fabrics.

Polyvinyl chloride (PVC) a plastic derived from oil or natural gas, and available in both rigid and flexible forms.

Rococo stitch a group of four vertical stitches, each spread apart and caught down at the centre to produce a rhomboid shape. Set in overlapping rows, leaving a tiny gap between each, they produce a mesh pattern.

Sarsenet in the seventeenth and eighteenth centuries, a light silk fabric.

Sealskin the seal's skin, complete with the fur dyed brown, and shaved to resemble fine velvet.

Shagreen in the late seventeenth century, a type of fishskin. In the early eighteenth century the skin was often ground smooth, leaving a distinctive pattern of small circles.

Spangle a small flat ornament, usually a metal disc, sewn on fabric for decoration.

Suede leather finished with a nap on the flesh side.

Taffeta a lightweight, lustrous silk.

Tambour work chain stitch embroidery, using a hooked needle to loop the thread through from the wrong side. Worked on a frame shaped like a drum (Fr. *tambour*).

Tapestry woven fabric a woven, ribbed cloth in which the weft is not continuous, different wefts being used for each area of pattern. Allows the weaving of complex patterns in imitation of embroidery.

Tent stitch rows of short parallel stitches, usually worked diagonally over one warp and one weft thread of the canvas, to give a firm, even covering.

Ticking stout cotton twill fabric, usually in narrow black and white stripes.

Vandyck trimming zig-zag edgings, supposedly imitating the pointed lace collars and cuffs of the seventeenth century, as painted by Sir Anthony van Dyck.

Whitework embroidery in white thread on white fabric, often using cut or drawn threads from the fabric to create areas of openwork and lace effects.

Worsted fine, long-fibre wool, highly spun to give a smooth, tightly twisted yarn.

Museums to Visit

Bath	Museum of Costume, Assembly Rooms, Bennett Street.
London	Museum of London, London Wall, EC2.
	Victoria and Albert Museum, South Kensington, SW7.
Manchester	The Gallery of English Costume, Platt Hall, Rusholme, Manchester 14.
Northampton	Museum of Leathercraft, Bridge Street.
Nottingham	Museum of Costume and Textiles, 51 Castlegate.
York	The Castle Museum.
Worthing	Worthing Museum and Art Gallery, Chapel Road.
Bristol	Blaise Castle House Museum, Henbury.
Cardiff	Welsh Folk Museum, St Fagans.
Glasgow	Museum of Costume Aikenhead House, King's Park, 325 Carmunnock Road.
Leeds	Lotherton Hall, Aberford.

Index